S. Hrg. 102–545

FOREVER YOUNG: MUSIC AND AGING

HEARING

BEFORE THE

SPECIAL COMMITTEE ON AGING
UNITED STATES SENATE

ONE HUNDRED SECOND CONGRESS

FIRST SESSION

WASHINGTON, DC

AUGUST 1, 1991

Serial No. 102–9

Printed for the use of the Special Committee on Aging

U.S. GOVERNMENT PRINTING OFFICE

48–782   WASHINGTON : 1992

For sale by the U.S. Government Printing Office
Superintendent of Documents, Mail Stop: SSOP, Washington, DC 20402-9328
ISBN 0-16-038346-3

CONTENTS

FOREVER YOUNG: MUSIC AND AGING

THURSDAY, AUGUST 1, 1991

U.S. SENATE,
SPECIAL COMMITTEE ON AGING,
Washington, DC.

The Committee met, pursuant to notice, at 10:20 a.m. in room 216, Hart Senate Office Building, Hon. Harry Reid [acting chairman of the Committee] presiding.

Present: Senators Reid, Cohen, Grassley, Burns, and Pressler, and Pryor [via satellite].

OPENING STATEMENT OF SENATOR HARRY REID, ACTING CHAIRMAN

Senator REID. Good morning everyone.

Welcome this morning to this hearing of the Special Committee on Aging. We are meeting to consider a topic never before directly raised by Congress: The therapeutic value of music.

Some may ask, and have asked, and justifiably so, what is so important about music? Isn't it simply entertainment or recreation? In fact, today's witnesses will tell us that music can work like medicine. Simply put, music can heal people.

Music is not only therapeutic, it is inexpensive.

Government does not have a lot of money to spare these days for new programs. Whenever a worthy solution is offered for a major problem, someone always interrupts, "How much is it going to cost?" Music therapy is an innovative approach that won't widen the deficit, but can help millions of older Americans live happier, more fulfilling lives. And we really can get these impressive results, as the saying goes, "for a song."

Before I complete my opening statement, though, I am pleased that we will have with us this morning the full chairman of this Special Committee on Aging. He will talk to us today via satellite from his office in Little Rock, AR. Incidentally, this is the first time in Senate history that a Senator makes an opening statement before a committee by satellite.

Senator David Pryor, who is widely recognized as one of the Nation's foremost leaders on issues of concern to the elderly, suffered a heart attack earlier this year. He has been sorely missed by all of us. We are pleased to have the chairman participate this morning.

Hello, David.

STATEMENT OF SENATOR DAVID PRYOR CHAIRMAN (VIA SATELLITE)

Senator PRYOR. Harry, good morning to you.

I'm standing in front of the Federal Building in Little Rock, AR. The temperature here today is expected to be at 102 degrees, so already this morning it is getting rather hot.

We have just had the State bird with us—I'm sorry he left. The mockingbird has been with us this morning here out in front of the Federal Building. We thought for the benefit of all those in the audience we'd give a little free concert here and, while talking about music, I thought we'd talk about the contributions the mockingbird has made.

It has now been about 3 months since I have been in Washington, as Senator Reid has said. Harry has been just wonderful to chair the hearings. He and his staff are doing a wonderful job. We want to thank you all, and owe your people, and all your staff people, a debt of gratitude for the preparation.

We want to make certain that this hearing is the first of its kind. We are going to explore some pioneer territory this morning in Washington.

The witnesses that you have assembled for this hearing are going to be those witnesses with a great deal of hands-on experience and real day-to-day living with those individuals with Alzheimer's, stroke, and with other disease and illness, where the music has played and can play such a critical and important role.

A wonderful panel has come from a long way, from across the country to attend this unique hearing this morning. We want to thank everyone for your participation.

Once again, I am reminded, through my own experience, that it is not just exercise and it is not just changing your lifestyle, it is not just hospitals and good doctors and good nurses and good friends, but it is something else that we must have and that we are looking for constantly in the system of health care delivery.

When we turn to music, we think music can do it. It is playing a very critical new and expanded role in not only providing for the psychological and emotional aspects of being sick or being old or having Alzheimer's, but also to trigger good memories and to trigger positive and constructive thoughts.

Let me turn this back over to Harry, once again thanking our panel. I'm sorry I couldn't be there. I will be watching the video, listening to the witnesses, and hearing all of what you have to say.

Thank you once again. Have a good time. Learn a lot. You're going to share some experiences. Thank you very much.

Senator REID. Thank you, David.

We will hear that for many older Americans music can increase alertness, physical vigor, and their capacity to continue meaningful relationships. Thousands of older Americans and those with disabilities are learning that music therapy improves their lives. They find it reaches further than traditional medications. According to 90-year-old Ida Goldman, who is seated before me, "Music is better than medicine."

Like medicine, music must be used properly to get results. This simple idea has been recognized for thousands of years.

Sir Francis Bacon explained to the King of England in the 17th century:

The poets did well to conjoin music and medicine because the office of medicine is but to tune this curious harp of man's body and to reduce it to harmony.

Today we can use scientific methods to examine and define how to use music as medicine. This hearing will document the current state of research in this relatively new field of scientific inquiry. We will also hear from people who have had remarkable experiences with music therapy.

You may wonder, "What is music therapy?" We don't often think of music as something used in a clinic. Yet, there are 5,000 certified music therapists across the country, some of whom are with us here today. They use carefully selected musical activities in hospitals, nursing homes, senior centers, rehabilitation centers, and other institutions. These therapists are well trained to assess people's needs and to apply the right activities to improve their physical, mental, or emotional lives.

Witnesses today will testify that Alzheimer's patients who have lost the ability to talk or to relate to their loved ones can still sing or dance. I know this because a former staffer of mine, Dana Gentry, has a grandmother in Las Vegas who suffers from Alzheimer's. Dana tells me she mumbles incoherently, and doesn't even know she is in a nursing home. But something special happens with music. I'd like to read to you from a letter that Dana wrote to me last week:

I love Grandma deeply and feel robbed by whatever demon has stolen her mind. Reaching back through the years I thought of the times when she held me in her arms and sang to me. Kneeling beside her wheelchair, I sang 'our song' directly into her ear.

At first it was just a slight glimmer of recognition that I noticed on her face. I was thrilled by that. And then she joined in. She sang the entire song, every word, and in harmony. And in the end, as tears rolled down my cheeks, she cried too, as if, for the moment, she realized her accomplishment.

We sing at every visit now. Sometimes when she sings I have her back, if only till the end of the song.

Dana's story illustrates a point. No, music cannot cure Alzheimer's victims, but new research demonstrates it can keep their minds awake and lift a veil of sadness from their families.

Dr. Oliver Sacks will tell us of "awakenings" that occur from music in Parkinson's and other neurologically afflicted patients. The film "Awakenings," based on Dr. Sacks' book, delivers this message, one that deserves our attention.

Dr. Sacks, I watched your movie last Saturday with my family, and it was a hit.

Two of America's top performers will give us their perspective on music's potential as a healing tool. Mickey Hart, drummer for the Grateful Dead for the past 25 years, and author of a recent book on the history of drumming, will share his insight. Theodore Bikel, a star on Broadway and in motion pictures, as well as a fabulous folk singer—that's where I first heard Theodore Bikel—will explain how music can keep us vibrant at any age.

Today's hearing raises a question: Do we need further research into music therapy? I think we do, because early evidence indicates that it serves those suffering from Alzheimer's disease and related dementias, strokes, depression, and other disabling conditions. Music therapy is a new field that shows great promise. Older persons may well benefit from further research.

Healthy older persons can also benefit from music. Dr. Frank Wilson will explain that older persons can learn to make music at any time in life. In fact, learning to play an instrument can keep older persons alert and creative.

Music has a positive impact on many people, from those in the best of health to those with severe neurological disorders. The Federal Government's concern is with those who are most vulnerable. Elderly and disabled individuals deserve Congress' attention. Congress can also remind our older citizens that learning music has rewards at any age.

The goal of this hearing is to discover what is known about music's role in the survival of human vitality. We will learn that music helps all types of people to remain "forever young."

Senator REID. Senator Cohen.

STATEMENT OF SENATOR WILLIAM COHEN

Senator COHEN. Thank you very much, Mr. Chairman.

As members of the audience may have detected, these beepers that are going off have just announced that a vote is underway, so I'm going to be very brief in my comments.

I'd like to extend my congratulations to Senator Pryor. This is the first time I have seen him since his heart attack. We have been reading about him in articles authored by him telling of his experience and some of the lessons he has learned in going through that traumatic experience of suffering a major heart attack.

Mr. Chairman, you mentioned the poets. I remember reading Shakespeare, who said that "Music can minister to minds diseased, pluck from the memory a rooted sorrow, raise out the written troubles of the brain, and with its sweet, oblivious antidote, cleanse the full bosom of all perilous stuff which weighs upon the heart." So I think that poets for years and years have recognized the importance of music to the spirit.

Mrs. Goldman, when the chairman mentioned that you were 90 years old—I have an 82-year-old father who still works 18 hours a day. I go back on weekends to work in his bakery. The thing that we enjoy most is listening to jazz every Sunday. He digs out his old tapes and records, and the two of us just sit there listening to some of the giants of the music world, going back to jazz at the Philharmonic. I can't begin to express to the people who are here what that does when I see him and the light that comes on in his eyes when we listen to that music together. So I am personally fully aware of the therapeutic value of music.

This is not only for older people. There is an experiment going on in Japan. I don't know the name offhand of the physician, but for years now he has been playing music to the fetus in pregnant women, and they have found there are extraordinary results coming from that with early development for multilingual opportunities. They develop much more rapidly than those without the benefit of that music having been played during that time. That's something that I want to explore at a later hearing.

Let me conclude by welcoming all of our witnesses here today and simply say that I believe that music, indeed, does rescue the heart from despair—particularly those who are confined to institutions, to those who may have suffered the loss of a spouse, the loss of their independence, and the loss of their homes. Music can play a very important role in rescuing that heart from despair.

Thank you very much, Mr. Chairman.

[The prepared statements of Senator Cohen, Senator Kohl, and Senator Simpson follow:]

OPENING STATEMENT OF SENATOR WILLIAM S. COHEN

Mr. Chairman, thank you for convening this hearing to explore ways that music can be used as therapy to improve the health and quality of life of older Americans.

Music has long been recognized for its special therapeutic and healing powers. William Shakespeare was reflecting on the value of music as therapy when he observed that:

"(Music) * * * can minister to minds diseased,
Pluck from the memory a rooted sorrow,
Raise out the written troubles of the brain,
And with its sweet, oblivious antidote,
Cleanse the full bosom of all perilous stuff
Which weighs upon the heart * * *."

As the Chairman noted, Dr. Oliver Sacks will be testifying before the Committee later this morning. In his book, *Awakenings*, he tells us that the "power of music to integrate and cure * * * is quite fundamental," and that music served as the "profoundest non-chemical medication" for his patients.

This will not come as news to any of our panelists or to the music therapists in our audience. Today, music therapy is a well-established, research-based profession, with over 5,000 certified music therapists practicing nationwide. Music therapists practice in a variety of settings such as hospitals, rehabilitation centers, nursing homes and senior centers. Through the carefully structured use of music, music therapists are able to help elderly and disabled individuals improve not only their mental and physical functioning, but their quality of life as well.

Quality health care encompasses not simply medical treatment, but also a basic understanding and respect for the patient as an individual and a human being. The creative opportunities provided by music therapists are particularly valuable for residents of nursing homes and other long-term care facilities. Music therapy can help to counteract the feelings of apathy and despair which are routinely experienced by long-term care patients coping with the loss of their independence, their homes, and often their spouses or friends. Such feelings of despair can defeat the efforts of the most understanding and hard-working health care personnel and can frustrate the entire purpose of the facility which is to maintain and improve the mental and physical well-being of the residents to the greatest possible extent.

Mr. Chairman, once again I commend you for convening what promises to be a most interesting hearing, and I look forward to the upcoming testimony.

STATEMENT OF SENATOR KOHL

Mr. Chairman: I would like to thank you and your staff for bringing together such an outstanding group of people for today's hearing. I must admit that I knew very little about music therapy before Senator Reid announced plans to hold this hearing. But over the past month, I have received many letters from music therapists from Wisconsin, each describing how music therapy can make a difference in the lives and therapeutic progress of older Americans.

I was especially moved by a letter from Wiltrud Hubbard, a registered music therapist at St. Anne's Home for the Elderly in Milwaukee. I wish that I could include in the hearing record a wonderful photograph that Ms. Hubbard sent to me that shows St. Anne's band at their July 4th concert. Ms. Hubbard explained that the band includes many who have showed marked improvement after joining the group, including a 100 year old woman who loves to play the clavichord and who won't even allow a visit from her family to interfere with her music sessions. St. Anne's band also includes a woman with advanced Alzheimer's who has learned to play the maracas. When this woman entered St. Anne's a year and a half ago, she did not want to go anywhere or do anything; with the help of music therapy, she now plays the maracas like a professional, with a smile on her face all the while.

There is so much that we can learn from our witnesses today about using music therapy as a tool to improve the lives and health of our nation's senior citizens. I am delighted that the Aging Committee is examining such a promising subject today, and I deeply appreciate Senator Reid's leadership in raising Congressional and public awareness about the value and potential of music therapy and the tremendous work of our nation's music therapists.

STATEMENT OF SENATOR ALAN K. SIMPSON

Good morning, Mr. Chairman. Your timing is very good—with all the thrashing around we have been doing on and off the Senate floor these last two weeks, you have provided us a delightful reprieve. I understand that today we will hear testimony of a sort not often offered up at these committee hearings—stories with a happy ending, stories that testify to hope and promise rather than high drama—doom and gloom. I, for one, am most appreciative.

"Music therapy"—not a field many of us are familiar with. I have reviewed the materials you provided earlier (and I appreciate that, too * * *) and I am intrigued. As many of my colleagues know, I have an interest in the subject of age-related dementias that is of a very personal and intimate nature. My own dear father resides in a nursing home in Cody, Wyoming. I visit him; it is extraordinarily painful to watch this marvelous man whom I love so dearly slip away—physically and mentally. That is just an extraordinarily difficult thing. My dear mother is 91 this month and is doing fairly well. My amazing mother-in-law is 91. So my wife Ann and I know something of this subject!

So I can appreciate the hope and the excitement of those who believe they have found a new way to reach those people who have what the clinicians call "dementia". I am a bit of a skeptic by nature—but I would surely wish to know more about this field called "music therapy." I look forward to hearing of your stories—and your successes. Thank you.

Senator REID. Senator Grassley.

STATEMENT OF SENATOR CHARLES GRASSLEY

Senator GRASSLEY. Mr. Chairman, I have got more to learn from this hearing probably than anybody else. I used to sing in church on Sunday until people would turn around to see who was singing behind them. I soon got the message that I probably don't sing very well.

You know, the true value is probably something that we all have to learn here, and I'm glad to know that music is very instrumental in helping people this way.

I am sorry that I was late. I was involved in other business. But my staff tells me that the introduction was a perfect demonstration of the power of music to affect people.

The letter you read from Dana Gentry was moving and a very good introduction for this hearing.

The topic that we take up today is a very interesting one, even for this Committee which has taken up many interesting topics over the years that I have been a member of it. The size of this crowd demonstrates the interest, as well as the importance, of this hearing, as well, as we have a very good turn-out.

I think exploration of this topic will expand all of our horizons. I have said how I think it is going to help me a great deal.

I understand that it seems pretty clear that music can be very effective as therapy, or as an aid to therapy, for ill and disabled older people, and can be a help and an inspiration to older people who are well.

I was particularly interested to learn from reading in preparation for this hearing that music can be very helpful in getting older people to exercise. I suppose that this is obvious when you think about it, but its importance may not be generally realized.

I was interested in this because a recent report by the Institute of Medicine called "The Second 50 years" contains a number of health promotion recommendations which, if followed, would enable older people to achieve and sustain better health and well-being. Among their recommendations was that exercise continues to be important at an older age in maintaining good health.

Of course, I realize that this is just one of many important things that can be accomplished through music. I think that this hearing will have done a service, even if the only thing it does is help to spread the idea that music should become a bigger part of the lives of older people in whatever setting they may find themselves.

If this Committee can help more concretely by finding ways to encourage settings such as nursing homes and senior centers and congregate meal sites use some music in some of the ways our witnesses will describe today, then I say so much the better.

I am looking forward to the testimony of our witnesses today, Mr. Chairman.

Senator REID. Thank you, Senator Grassley.

We have some votes pending. Senator Cohen has left and is going to try to get back in time to get me over to vote.

Mrs. Goldman, please proceed with your testimony. We'll do our best to be as attentive as possible. We greatly appreciate your waiting through all these opening statements.

STATEMENT OF MRS. IDA GOLDMAN, ROCKVILLE, MD

Mrs. GOLDMAN. [Videotape presentation.]

Mr. Chairman and members of this Committee, my name is Ida Goldman. I'm 90 years old. I live at the Hebrew Home of Greater Washington in Rockville, MD. I'm happy to have a chance to talk to you about one of my favorite subjects—music.

I like to sing. I like to dance. And all day long I hum my favorite tunes, one song after another. Music makes my day.

This past spring, our music therapist, Kathy Mollard, directed our own version of "South Pacific." The music was beautiful, and everyone seemed to enjoy the show. For the first time, we had six high school students play a part in the show. They were from the Churchill High School in Gaithersburg. I like it when we have two generations working together.

It makes me happy to know that I am able to entertain other people. I sang "I'm Gonna Wash That Man Right Outta My Hair." The beautiful music in the show was therapy to the people in the show, as well as for the audience.

Music is better than medicine. I know that for a fact. Before I had surgery, they told me I would never walk again. I had terrible pain in my leg and back. I couldn't even close my hand. But when I sat and listened to the music, I forgot all about the pain. When I listen to the music—any kind of music—I don't think of anything else. My whole mind is only on the music I hear.

I even dance to the music. My toes just start tapping away every time I hear music—even in a restaurant. I like all kinds of music, and the waltz music is my favorite.

Part of the therapy of music is that it brings many memories from past years. I can remember when my mother used to sing Yiddish songs to me. She sang to us all the time. I love to think of the song that my husband sang to me—and you just heard that—"Let me call you Sweetheart." My grandson, Daniel, just won a big award for playing the drum. It is a changing world, but one thing that never changes is music.

We have a lot of music in our home. My friend, Joe Arnoff, plays for us on every Saturday afternoon for 2 hours, Monday for 1 hour. He just started playing music for us Friday evening. He plays waltzes, classical music, and many of the singers. He plays big band music to give us a lift.

Samuel Rogow plays his harmonica in the lobby every day. He can play almost any song. He's an invalid. He is in a wheelchair.

Our music therapist, Kathy Mollard, plays the piano beautifully. She plays for us every Thursday night, and she plays music on every floor in the Hebrew Home—and that's four floors. She works at it all week long.

The people in our hand bell choir play beautifully. Some of the people are in very poor health, but they can still make pretty music.

Kathy and Anita help us put on a musical every year. I have been in "Annie Get your Gun," "Oliver," "Oklahoma," "Wizard of Oz," and "South Pacific." I'm looking forward to making my next big hit next year. I hope you can all come and see it because I am inviting every one of you.

I really don't feel my age. I feel like a youngster. I get younger every day.

Senator REID. Thank you, Mrs. Goldman.

Would you please proceed, Mrs. Johnson?

STATEMENT OF LOIS JOHNSON, McDONALD, KS

Mrs. JOHNSON. Mr. Chairman and members of this Committee, I want to thank you for this opportunity to let me tell you about music therapy as I witnessed it with my husband and other patients with dementia of the Alzheimer type.

My name is Lois Johnson. I am from McDonald, KS. I'm sure you are wondering where McDonald is. McDonald is a small town in northwest Kansas—150 people. I own and operate the only retail business in town—a small grocery store.

I'd like to tell you a little bit about the disease as it happened to us. My husband, Tom, was only 48 years old. He managed a small grain elevator, a job he thoroughly loved, and I managed the small grocery store. Our last three kids left for college, and our first grandchild was on the way. We felt things were just looking very good for us.

Tom was always a very great family man. He never missed many events that his children performed in. Many times we would go to one town and watch his sons perform in ballgames, and drive to another college and watch our daughter perform in a dance drill team. Tom was a very proud father.

He was also very proud to be a volunteer fireman. He was very skilled with his hands. He remodeled our home several times. He made lots of gifts for his children and his friends. He could repair anything from a motor to a car. And he was also quite a prankster. I remember one time he delivered a 2-ton rock, put it on his brother's front door step, and then put an ad in the local paper advertising a pet rock for sale. These were his pet jokes.

But slowly this nightmare began. We first noticed that he would make any excuse to avoid going to a sporting event, or a family get-together, or anything that had a lot of people involved. He became more and more withdrawn. His jokes and his puns became more of the cruel kind. He would go up to people and tell them "You're getting very fat," or "You're getting bald headed," or "You sure are getting grey."

I can remember he started pinching and pulling hair, and it didn't seem to matter if he knew the people or not.

One day the fire whistle blew, and Tom actually hid to keep from going to the fire.

Suddenly one day he came up to me and he announced he had quit his job. I said, "How in the world do you intend to pay the bills?" He just looked at me and he said, "You can do it." That seemed to be his answer to everything at that time—you can do it.

Tom had always been an affectionate, caring person, but now we noticed that he was becoming more and more withdrawn. He retreated to bed every chance he got, as though he could sleep away all the bad things that were happening to him. One son came home from college one vacation, and he said, "Mom, all I see in Dad's eyes is blankness." The kids were noticing a big change in their father.

Our youngest daughter lived with us at this time. She was waiting for her first teaching job to open up. She came to me one day and she said, "Mom, I just can't stand this tormenting any longer. I'm going to have to move out before I hate my Dad." I well understood what she meant, but can you imagine the terrible feelings we were going through?

To me this just seemed like a nightmare that had no end.

Two years passed before we got a diagnosis. Several months of this time Tom spent in a mental hospital. When we finally got the diagnosis, Tom was no longer the person that we used to have. He became a stranger needing constant care and constant supervision. But we now had some answers to the strange things that had been happening.

A dementia of this type attacks the short-term memory bank first. And the first things to go are their personality and their social graces. I often refer to this as the death of a personality, because that's exactly what is happening. You are losing them in stages, and the personality is the very first.

Slowly everything else disappears and they return to total infancy. When I could no longer take care of Tom I took him to the veterans' hospital in Topeka, KS. This was 300 miles from our home. I did go visit him several days each month, but by this time Tom was so agitated he could no longer sit or sleep—only for brief periods of time. I resorted to walking the hallways with him.

There was no recognition left that I could see. He could no longer speak—not even one word. And I could no longer get eye contact with him.

I noticed that Tom developed what I called the "caged animal" syndrome. He was always full of fear, always seeming to be fleeing from something, but he didn't know what. On three different occasions he eloped from the locked-door ward.

After Tom had been ill for about 6 years the VA called me and they said that Dr. Clair had selected Tom to be a student in her music therapy for the Alzheimer's patient. My first thought, I have to admit, was very selfish. I said, "Good. They are going to have to keep him at least 2 more months and I'm not going to have to worry about what to do with him." My second thought was, "What in the world do they hope to accomplish? Here is a man that can't even speak."

The first few sessions went just as I had thought they would. Tom would not sit still, he would not participate. If they handed him an instrument, he simply laid it on the floor. But I went back several weeks later and a wonderful thing was happening. Dr. Clair was sitting in front of Tom. She had eye contact. She was holding his hands. She was singing to him. And Tom was making sounds in his throat as though he was trying to respond. I just couldn't believe it. I even saw him reach toward a guitar and strum it.

He played the maracas in a way that was only him. He would touch her knee, he would touch his head, and then his knee. He did this in repetitious movement for as long as the music played.

I could see tears in Tom's eyes whenever the patriotic songs or the hymns were played. The thrill of seeing just a little bit of the man that I used to know was just overwhelming.

I knew that Tom could never get well, but music opened up a window to his soul that I just so badly needed at that time.

I also observed changes in other dementia patients. One patient that had not spoken a complete sentence for a long time stood up and sang a jazz song from start to finish without missing a beat.

My daughter is a registered nurse, and she tells of a patient in her care that is very violent and aggressive, but his daughters can come and sing to him and he calms right down.

My mother developed a malignant brain tumor at the same time that Tom was sick. She returned also to her childhood, but we used music as a way to keep her calm, too.

During the last several months of Tom's life he became the infant that I told you about. He became totally bedfast, needing constant care. Everything had to be done for him. But there was in his eyes something you can't imagine.

Music therapy gave me one last key to reaching that past-term memory that I so badly needed at this time. I could always reach Tom with music. I could take his hands, get eye contact, sing a slow, soothing song, and the fear would simply leave his eyes.

One day, in particular, Tom seemed more aware. I can remember that afternoon that I sang the song "Amazing Grace" to him several times. I'm not a musician. That just happened to be the only song I could remember the words to. I left the hospital later that evening, and within the hour they called and said that Tom had passed away.

Music gave me some moments that I will always remember, and I know that it gave him peace.

I do not believe that music therapy can cure the dementia, but I do believe that it can reach a part of the past-term memory that other things cannot reach. And anything that can stimulate this brain can hold off the disease maybe just a little longer and give them a little bit more peace.

I am convinced that music therapy is a very important link to the past for the Alzheimer's patient and for their families, as it was for us.

After my husband was diagnosed with Pick's disease, a severe dementia related to Alzheimer's, I was invited to serve on the Governor's Task Force for Alzheimers and related diseases in the State of Kansas. I continued to serve as a spokeswoman from 1985 to 1989.

During this time, I testified within hearings that resulted in legislation that provided some support and help for patients and families. The "Helpline" was installed in the Department of Aging. Insurance for long-term care was improved to include people diagnosed with Alzheimer's disease. A Division of Assets bill was passed to help the spouse of a long-term care patient.

I continue to give workshops in Kansas and Colorado to nursing home staff and family members about coping with a long-term degenerative disease.

I appreciate your scheduling a hearing about music therapy and giving me a chance to share my views. Thank you.

STATEMENT OF SENATOR CONRAD BURNS

Senator BURNS. Thank you, Mrs. Johnson. That's a very touching story.

Not too far from where you live we are experiencing the same thing with my wife's father in North Platte, NE. We are experiencing what you and your family have experienced.

Here's a man that was born on that ranch, raised all of his kids on that ranch, and in the same house, and now he can't find the bathroom.

Mrs. JOHNSON. Right.

Senator BURNS. When you were going through those times, did you have any resource of a support group or another person?

Mrs. JOHNSON. I had nothing. Tom was diagnosed at a time that Alzheimer's was very, very unknown. There was one book written, "The 36-hour day." I started to read it, and it was so clinical and so depressing I never did finish it. We had never even heard the word. But in our town of 150 people, they actually took care of my husband while I worked.

Senator BURNS. You are still living in McDonald?

Mrs. JOHNSON. I still live in McDonald.

Senator BURNS. I may have my mother-in-law call you.

Mrs. JOHNSON. I would appreciate that. I work a lot with Alzheimer's patients and their families. I have support groups. I do teaching in nursing homes. I'd be most happy to talk to her.

Senator BURNS. Because it is a terrible thing.

Your husband responded to music when he was at the VA hospital.

Mrs. JOHNSON. That's right.

Senator BURNS. Did you note if other patients also responded to music?

Mrs. JOHNSON. Very much so. The man that I spoke of that sang the jazz song was in his group. Twice a year they would have a dance for the patients and invite the spouses. You'd be amazed at the people that could hardly walk that could get up and dance.

Senator BURNS. We got to taking a resource count in my State. I think we only have six music therapists in the whole State of Montana. Those of you that are not from Montana, it is 148,000 square miles, but we are only 800,000 people. Would you advocate some sort of Federal help in this area?

Mrs. JOHNSON. I certainly would. If you can't get enough of the music therapists, themselves, I see no reason they couldn't teach the activity directors, and also teach them in the way that is effective. I have seen music in nursing homes, but it has a beat, it has a lot of background. This doesn't work. You need something more calming, something more direct, and they need to learn this. I think music therapy teachers could teach the activity directors.

Senator BURNS. Unknowingly, on the other hand, my parents, who are still living in northwest Missouri—we celebrated their 60th wedding anniversary the other day—both of them are still living in their own home and keeping their own garden, going on like they don't even know they are old.

Mrs. JOHNSON. Wonderful.

Senator BURNS. Quite a lot like Mrs. Goldman. Two or three years ago, my mother used to play the piano. She couldn't read music very well. She always played by ear. In fact, she learned at a theater where they had silent film. We gave her one of these little electric pianos. She plays it all the time, and it is great therapy.

Mrs. JOHNSON. Wonderful therapy.

Senator BURNS. And so I take your words as very weighty words here. We appreciate your coming today.

Mrs. Goldman, the residents of Hebrew Home where you live can participate in music every day. Would you say that's very important to their daily routine?

Mrs. GOLDMAN. Very important. There are a lot of invalids there.

Senator BURNS. Do you think music therapy should be offered to residents in other homes like yours across this Nation?

Mrs. GOLDMAN. We have a resident that is an invalid, and he plays music for us every Saturday afternoon for 2 hours, and he plays 1 hour on Monday mornings, and now he started playing for us every Friday night. We have a ball. It is sing along, mostly. And then we have this young lady next to me, Kathy, who plays beautiful music for us on Thursday nights. She plays the records, but she does play the piano. We just love it. It seems that everyone became alive. But, as far as myself, I grow younger every day and love it.

Another thing I want to say is that the world is changing, but music will never change.

Thank you all for coming to hear me.

Senator BURNS. It is our pleasure coming to hear you. I have always been a little bit of a philosopher, myself, and I have always said that music and humor cures more than pills or hypodermic needles. I still believe that. So we thank you three young ladies for coming to this Committee today. I'll turn it back to my chairman, Senator Reid.

[The prepared statement of Senator Burns follows:]

PREPARED STATEMENT OF SENATOR CONRAD BURNS

Mr. Chairman, I want to thank you for scheduling this hearing today on Music and the Aging.

Looking at those here that will be testifying and all the folks that have come to listen, it is obvious to me that music plays a great part in our lives, both for the young and the aging. I know that I can easily relieve stress, brighten my day or just remember a happy occasion by listening to the right music. It makes perfect sense that this should be the case for older Americans, especially those with special needs.

I thank all of you for being with us here today. And I commend you for your energy—it's contagious and inspiring. I look forward to hearing your testimony and enjoying the performances to come.

Senator REID. Senator Burns, thank you very much.

Ladies, thank you very much for being here today.

We will now have as our next witness Dr. Oliver Sacks from New York City.

Dr. Sacks, would you come forward please?

This is Robin Williams in disguise.

Dr. SACKS. Advanced version.

STATEMENT OF OLIVER SACKS, M.D., NEW YORK, NY

Dr. SACKS. Mr. Chairman and members of the Committee, I first want to express my gratitude for being allowed to testify before you today.

I submitted some written testimony, but I think I may wing it.

Senator REID. That testimony that has been submitted in writing will be made part of the record. Please do wing it.

Dr. SACKS. A century ago Nietzsche, the philosopher, wrote some fascinating notes on physiology and art. In particular, he spoke of the powers of music. He talked of these as being dynamic, tonic, mnemonic, concentrating, communicating, and liberating. He quoted an aphorism of Novalis, the poet, that all diseases are musical problems and all cures are musical solutions. He also said "When we listen to music we listen with our muscles."

I think these insights have been clarified and confirmed and illustrated by our experience in these days.

I work especially with older patients in chronic hospitals of various sorts, and neurological disabilities are particularly common among such patients—especially Parkinson's disease, strokes, and Alzheimer's disease. Together, these affect more than 10 million people in this country.

I should add that I have also worked with populations of autistic and retarded people, and also with psychotic populations who can be greatly helped by music, but I will confine myself to speaking of the older populations with physical and neurological disabilities.

I am constantly struck by the fact that, though medicine cannot offer some of these patients any decisive cure, their neurological functioning, no less than their morale, can be immensely improved by therapeutic measures of a nonmedical sort—especially by human contact, by art, and, above all, by music therapy.

This can be equally true of elderly patients who have had orthopedic mishaps. Their rehabilitation is never a purely surgical matter. They have to get back that total integration of movement and posture which they had before the injury.

Let me give you an example.

I saw one patient, an old lady who had had a complex hip fracture which required surgery and immobilization with a cast. Her leg hadn't recovered after this. It was apparently paralyzed and useless, although no orthopedic reason was clear for this.

I asked her if her leg had ever moved. She thought for a bit, and she said yes, there was a Christmas concert a year back and when an Irish jig was played her foot kept time. So clearly her leg and some part of her was capable of responding to music.

Physiologically, we found a complete electrical silence in the muscles of her leg, and we couldn't find any "evoked potentials" in the leg areas of the brain. The leg was no longer being represented neurologically; yet, on occasion, it could respond to music.

Physiotherapy was of no help for this lady, but music therapy was of enormous help. We were able, after she told us this, to elicit rhythmic, automatic responses to music, first in the foot, then in the whole leg. Later we were able to get her to dance with support, and finally to walk.

I wish I could show you a tape of all of this, because it is an example of a permanent restoration of function which was made possible by music.

But my special experiences, as you referred to, are with post-encephalitic and Parkinsonian patients. In patients like this, there may be a good deal of muscular stiffness and rigidity. There is great difficulty initiating movement. There can be long periods of freezing and transfixion. There is an absence of spontaneity, and even when movement and speech are possible they tend to be feeble and rather lifeless and mechanical.

But such patients show an unimpaired ability to respond, whether it is to a thrown ball or, especially, to music. And one can see patients who, though unable to walk, are able to dance; and patients who, though unable to talk, are able to sing. At this stage, if it works, I'd like to show you a little bit of videotape from the documentary of "Awakenings."

[Videotape presentation.]

Dr. SACKS. You see how in singing the voice is transformed in this patient. It is usually flat and toneless and anonymous, but when she sings it has a full volume, a full tonality, a full emotional range. In another bit of this tape I don't have enough time to show you, you see this almost immobile patient able to dance, and in doing so to recover all of her animation.

I thought there was going to be more tape, but let me just mention another patient who is also in the documentary, another post-encephalitic patient, Rosalie, who often, for hours a day, would be totally transfixed, usually with a finger touching her spectacle lens. But as soon as we brought her to the piano—she loved playing—she would be transformed when she played. There was an ease and a fluency and a freedom and a normality which one never saw at any other time.

Not only did music liberate her from her Parkinsonism, but the imagining of music would do so. She knew all Chopin by heart, and all one had to do was to say "Opus 49" and immediately the F

Minor Fantasy would start playing in her mind and her rigidity would disappear, her facial expression would come back, and she could move easily.

And if one did an EEG—an electroencephalogram—at this time, the brain activity, which was normally of an almost coma-like slowness, would also become normal while she was playing or imagining music. So here, very strikingly, music was a cure—at least, restored her to normal cerebral and psychic function while it lasted.

This power of music to animate and to organize activity is most striking in patients with motor and motor-regulatory disorders like this. Music is not a luxury to such patients, it is a necessity. They cannot even move without it.

One such patient, who had been a former music teacher, spoke of herself as having been "unmusicked" by her Parkinsonism and as needing to be "remusicked" in order to move.

Equally important is the power of music to mobilize elderly patients who may have become immobile because of illness or depression or lethargy or pain or fear. Immobility is a great danger in such patients. It predisposes to everything from bed sores to dementia. Music can act as a tonic and get such patients going.

With regard to how it works, we can only speculate. The affected parts of the brain in Parkinsonism are the basal ganglia, which have been called the "organs of succession." If these are damaged, people have great difficulty with successions of movement, with consecutive movement.

But music can apparently substitute for this damaged brain function and become a template for organizing movement and for doing. To some extent, music can act instead of the basal ganglia, can act as a prosthesis for this damaged part of the brain.

This is not something mechanical. Patients don't react to any music, they have to have music they like, and music which moves them. This is true, in general, of music therapy. There is no such thing as "general" music. All music is particular, and it must accord with the tastes of each patient.

As music can substitute for lower functions, it can be vital in higher functions. In Alzheimer's disease, as you have heard, you can have patients who are unable to talk, unable to organize themselves, patients who are agitated and confused. Music for them can have an almost magical power by eliciting memories and associations and restoring to them the moods, the memories, the fluency, and the feeling of their former selves and their former lives.

Music perhaps is mostly dynamic in something like Parkinsonism, but it has an evocative and mnemonic power in patients with Alzheimer's disease, which can totally recall the lost person for a while, or rather give access to lost powers and lost identity—an access which cannot be provided by anything else. Here again, as with the brief awakening of post encephalitic patients, this restoration to self and to normality is accompanied by a temporary normalization in the EEGs.

In summary, though the nervous system is sometimes compared to a computer, I think it is much more like an orchestra or a symphony. I think we are musical through and through, from the lowest levels of rhythm in our nerve cells to the highest levels. There is a vast range of neurological disorders in which this inner music is impaired, and all of these can be transformed by the healing power of music.

Thank you.

[The prepared statement of Dr. Sacks follows:]

TESTIMONY OF DR. OLIVER SACKS, NEUROLOGIST

Neurological disabilities are particularly common in older age groups; this is especially so of strokes, Parkinson's disease, and Alzheimer's disease, which together affect more than ten million Americans over the age of 65, and often necessitate their admission to nursing homes and chronic hospitals. As a neurologist who has worked with such patients for 25 years, I am constantly struck by the fact that though Medicine cannot offer them any decisive cure, their physical and mental states, their functioning, can often be immensely improved by remedial and therapeutic measures of a nonmedical sort, for example by art therapy and most especially by music therapy. This may be equally true of elderly patients who have suffered broken hips and other orthopedic mishaps: the rehabilitation of such patients is not a purely surgical matter—they need to regain their former motor competence and confidence, that total automatic integration of movement and posture which they enjoyed before their injuries, and here too music can play a vital role.

Let me give you an example. One patient, typical of many, was an old lady with an apparently paralyzed and useless left leg. It had been like this since a complex hip fracture, followed by surgery, and weeks in a cast. Surgery had been successful, but her leg, strangely, remained inert and useless. The muscles of the leg, indeed, showed a complete "electrical silence," and "evoked potential" studies in the brain showed that it was no longer represented in the sensory areas, had completely dropped out of body-image—and yet it was a good leg, with no residual injury. Had the leg ever moved since the injury, I asked her? Yes, it had—it once "kept time" at a Christmas concert, when an Irish jig was being played. This showed that the leg could respond, could move, if there were the right, musical stimulus. Ordinary physiotherapy had been useless—could musical therapy accomplish what physiotherapy had failed to, we wondered? In fact, it did: we were able to elicit strong automatic ("entrained") responses to music and rhythm, to get her to make dancing movements, and finally to walk. I wish I could show you a tape of all this—the power of music in such a patient to effect a permanent restoration; but time is limited, and I must pass on to other examples.

My most concentrated experience, over the years—as some of you will know from the film or book of "Awakenings"—has been with post-encephalitic and parkinsonian patients. In these patients there may be much muscular stiffness and rigidity; there may be a peculiar difficulty in initiating any movement; there may be long "hang-ups" and "freezings" and "trances," in which patients get helplessly transfixed. There is an absence of spontaneity; and movement and speech, even when possible, tend to be feeble, and lacking in energy and life. And yet such patients shows an unimpaired ability to respond—and may do so, dramatically, in response to sudden emergencies, or a suddenly-thrown ball, or in response to appropriate music. The power of music is very remarkable in such patients—one sees parkinsonian patients unable to walk, but able to dance perfectly well; or patients almost unable to talk, who are able to sing perfectly well. I cannot bring a patient to show you, but I have brought a little videotape, excerpted from the documentary of "Awakenings."

(Show Tape Excerpt)

A motionless patient rises when music is played, and though still rigid, dances to it fluently. * * * The patient's low, flat, almost unintelligible voice is transformed when she sings "Just a song at twilight." It regains all its old volume and fluency; there is a complete return of all its emotional and vocal tone.

Here is another patient, Rosalie, who for hours a day tended to remain transfixed, completely motionless, stuck, usually with one finger on her spectacles. But she can play the piano beautifully, and for hours—and when she plays her parkinsonism disappears, and all is ease and fluency and freedom and normality. Music liberates her from her parkinsonism for a time—and not only music, but the imagining of music. Rosalie knows all Chopin by heart, and one has only to say "Opus 49!" to her for her whole body and posture and expression to change. Her parkinsonism vanishes, as the F-minor Fantasie plays itself in her mind; her electroencephalogram (EEG), usually of almost coma-like slowness, also changes, becomes completely normal—when she is playing (or even imagining) music. The power of music to animate and organize brain activity—Kant called it "the quickening art"—is particularly spectacular in patients like this who lack the normal ongoing motor and motor-regulatory activity the rest of us have. Music is not a luxury but a necessity to such patients, and can (for a while) provide them what their brains no longer provide.

The affected parts of the brain, in parkinsonism, are the basal ganglia, which have been called "the organs of succession." If they are damaged, patients have great difficulty with sequences, with consecutive movement—but music can substitute for this basal gangliar function, can become (while it lasts) a "template" for organizing a series of movements, for doing. This is not something mechanical—the music must "move" the patient emotionally, otherwise it will have no basal gangliar effect. So it is not sufficient, usually, to put on a loud rock band, or Muzak—there must be a sensitive exploration, first, of the kind of music which works for each patient. There is no "general" music—music is particular and it works, in the first place, by evoking a particular response, a particular appreciative and creative response, which can then translate itself into a specific physiological activation. This may be so even in other animals: thus studies by Otto Creutzfeldt at the Max-Planck-Institut in Gottingen, with multiple electrodes measuring brain activity, have shown that cats may be calmed or activated by music, and that music can bring about striking synchronizations and "entrainments" of brain function. The music which does this most powerfully is Mozart—all cats respond to Mozart (he is neurologically "correct"), though different cats respond best to different pieces by Mozart. Each cat, each brain, has its preference, its favorite—the one that works best for it.

As music can substitute for "lower" motor functions, organized in the spinal cord or basal ganglia, it can equally serve to stimulate and organize higher mental functions, especially when these have been damaged by disease. Many elderly patients with strokes are aphasic—they have lost some of their ability to articulate or use words; but the words which are lost may come back with singing, and music therapy can sometimes help the patient to adopt a sing-song way of speaking, a way which will hold sentence-structure in a matrix of music. Other patients may have a visual agnosia—an inability to organize, to make sense of the world visually. But such patients, like Dr. P., in my book, "The Man Who Mistook His Wife for a Hat", may be able to substitute music for seeing, to reorganize their activities and perceptions in musical terms, to hold themselves and their lives and their worlds together with music.

Finally, and most importantly: those patients—whose numbers now, tragically, run into the millions—those patients with a dementia due to the diffuse cortical damage of Alzheimer's disease, patients who may be in a pitiful state of agitation and confusion because their memories and powers to organize are failing, because they cannot hold themselves and their worlds together. The power of music is fundamental, with such patients, but it works in a different identity-restoring way. For the parkinsonian, music acts as a template for organizing movement, for doing; for the dement, it acts as (a sort of) Proustian mnemonic, eliciting emotions and associations which had been long forgotten, giving the patient access once again to moods and memories and thoughts and worlds which, seemingly, they had completely lost. One sees that it is not an actual loss of memories here, but a loss of access to these—and music, above all, can provide access once again, can constitute a key for opening the door to the past, a door not only to specific moods and memories, but to the entire thought-structure and personality of the past.

Thus with music—and here, above all, it must be the "right" music, the music which holds significance, has meaning for the individual—the demented patient can be restored to himself; can recall, re-access, not only his powers of speech, his perceptual and thinking skills, but his entire emotional and intellectual configuration, his life history, his identity—for a while. It is incredibly poignant to see such recalls, such restorations of the otherwise lost persona. I wish I could show you some of the extraordinary tapes which Connie Tomaino, our music therapist, has made of some patients; I wish indeed that she could be here today, for she could convey, much better than I could, the full wonder of these things.

In summary, though the nervous system is sometimes compared to a computer, it is really much more like a symphony or orchestra, in which everything must be synchronized, harmonized, melodized. There is, in health, an "implicit" music, which keeps the basal ganglia, the cortex, all parts of the brain, together—an implicit music rooted, first and foremost, in the rhythmicity of all nervous action and its tying-together, its entrainment, at more and more complex rhythmic levels. If, because of damage or disease, the nervous system is impaired in its sensory input or motor output, or its internal integrations in the basal ganglia or cerebral cortex, then this internal natural music is interfered with, and the need for an external music is overwhelming. There is a vast range of neurological (and neuropsychological) disorders—ranging from simple motor problems to parkinsonism to language and perceptual deficits, to dementia (to say nothing of such problems as autism, retardation, and depression)—in which the innter music of the organism (which Harvey, in 1627, called "the silent music of the body") is impaired; and all of these can be transformed, if only for a while, by the healing powers of music.

Senator REID. Dr. Sacks, I think that we need to pause and contemplate on what is going on here today. We have you, who just isn't someone who came in from the street with some ideas. You are a medically trained neurologist. As a result of the work which you did, which you wrote about and now which has been depicted in a movie, it has triggered people's imaginations so that people like Theodore Bikel and Mickey Hart, who are musicians and have known all their musical lives that this magic happens, you are now here trying to explain to us that it really does happen for some medical reasons. You should be congratulated for that.

Doctor Sacks, I watched the movie "Awakenings" the other night—and, by the way, I had read the book beforehand. If patients are immobile, inactive, and their muscles atrophy as was the case for those depicted in the movie, how could they get up and start walking and doing these things?

Dr. SACKS. In Parkinsonism there may be a lot of rigidity, and rigidity, itself, can prevent atrophy and act like a sort of isometric exercise.

Senator REID. Is that right?

Dr. SACKS. But also these patients had been walked passively, so they weren't totally immobile.

Senator REID. Dr. Sacks, how accurate was the movie?

Dr. SACKS. It had some romantic additions, but otherwise it was reasonably accurate.

Senator REID. I guess the point that I wanted to make is that you were a young physician going into this facility, and these patients were—and I, as all politicians, have been into some nursing homes. The facility depicted there is like many in Nevada that I have been in. You walked in there. Why did you throw the ball and have people reaching for it? What caused you to think that these people could be awakened?

Dr. SACKS. Well, there had been accounts and anecdotes of patients suffering with——

Senator REID. And you had studied this and remembered it; is that right?

Dr. SACKS. Well, the nurses would tell me about anecdotes. The nurses were wonderful. Some of them had been with the patients for 30 years, and so had therapists. And I sometimes saw this sudden action for myself.

Senator REID. For those in the audience that haven't seen the movie and don't know what we are talking about, people who had been asleep, in effect, sitting and staring off into space, when thrown a ball would reach up and grab the ball. Right?

Dr. SACKS. Yes. I think probably it was closer to a sort of trance-like state or a transfixion, a spellbound state, rather than sleep.

Senator REID. Anyway, why did you think that the work that you did would awaken these people, some of which was with music?

Dr. SACKS. Well, one saw in this transfixed state that there needed to be a drawing of attention out of their own sphere. Sometimes you would see a patient staring at the ground, and if you simply said to him, "Look over there," he could break out and look over there and maybe walk over there, but he couldn't do so alone. You had to call him.

So my first act before any medication became possible was to look at the different things which could call these patients out of their spellbound state. A very strong one was music.

Senator REID. Tell me, doctor, these people, during the time that they were awakened, did they have thought processes?

Dr. SACKS. Yes, indeed.

Senator REID. The movie depicted that these people were normal during the time that they were awake. They communicated. Is that, in fact, the case?

Dr. SACKS. Yes. It is very much the case. One had very much the feeling of the normal personality and normal intellectual powers and thought processes which had been imprisoned or transfixed and needed to be let out.

Senator REID. Now, Doctor, with the medication that you were giving these people—L–DOPA I think was the name of it—the positive effects of it diminished over time. With music is there that same diminishing effect?

Dr. SACKS. No. However deep the disability, I think the powers of music are always there and are permanent. And when the medicine wears off, music is still there. It employs a different physiological mechanism. In a way, it bypasses the Parkinsonism.

Senator REID. Senator Cohen.

Senator COHEN. Thank you very much.

Doctor Sacks, you indicated in your testimony that all music is particular. It is not universal in appreciation, as such. I think Mr. Hart is going to testify that percussion perhaps is universal. The people in the audience cannot see this, but hopefully if there is ever a replay of this hearing they will notice that while you were testifying your right foot was tapping, and you were perhaps not even aware of that. But, as you were responding to questions from Senator Reid, in particular, I noticed that you were tapping with your foot. So perhaps Mr. Hart can talk to us about the universality of percussion as far as music is concerned.

Of course, you were quoting Nietzsche. It goes back a lot further than Nietzsche. Plato talked about the music of the spheres and that the musicians were the ones closest in this whole hierarchy of development of the human being to the philosopher king. Next to the philosopher king were the musicians. I think there has been a recognition historically of the importance of music in our lives.

I was wondering—I have been doing some reading in a different field of the mind-body connection—some of the writings of Deepak Chopra, who was an Indian endocrinologist who talks about the powers of the mind to actually engage in the healing process, as well. There is more and more literature being disseminated on a very wide-scale basis, and I suspect this falls into the same category of the interconnectability of the mind in the healing process.

I was wondering about something. Would some patients or people be more responsive to visual stimulus or stimuli as opposed to music? Art, for example, versus music? Is there anything in your experience that would indicate that a visual experience is perhaps better for a particular patient?

Dr. SACKS. Well, certainly if patients are profoundly deaf then visual stimuli are all important, but I think other forms of art therapy are also crucial. People with Alzheimer's disease sometimes who are no longer able to speak or conceptualize can do beautiful art and can enjoy art. I think visual art is equally important for them.

Senator COHEN. Is it necessary to have any prior musical background for a patient to be responsive to it? Do they have to have either studied music in the past, had their parents force them to play the piano as they were growing up, as many of us were? Is there anything that goes back to prior experience? Can you have someone who has no experience other than perhaps listening to music as a teenager? Is anything required in the way of prior experience?

Dr. SACKS. I don't think any musical skill is required. I think musical responsiveness is universal, even in people who are sometimes called unmusical. Certainly responsiveness to rhythm is universal. Actually, that's not only in human beings, but also in many animals as well. There have been some fascinating physiological studies about the effects of music in cats. I should add that Mozart is most effective with cats.

Senator COHEN. Bach doesn't do as well?

Dr. SACKS. Apparently not.

Senator COHEN. With respect to therapy or therapists, is it their job and their experience to single out the kind of music that would be most applicable to that given individual? In other words, Bach might be okay, or Mozart, but maybe not Kenny G or maybe not the Grateful Dead.

Dr. SACKS. I think music therapy always has to occur in a human relationship. This will include exploring what the patient likes most and responds to most, and then perhaps expanding that.

Senator COHEN. Is there anything in your experience that leads you to the conclusion that music would make it possible for a permanent curative effect rather than a temporary response?

Dr. SACKS. Well, I think that Parkinsonian patients and patients with movement disorders can learn to imagine music and organize their own activity with it internally to a considerable extent. And I think sometimes with Alzheimer patients, once the doors have been opened they may remain open to a considerable extent. I think the last witness indicated that. So I think one definitely has some after effect.

Senator COHEN. The chairman and I were wondering how it came that you were able to make yourself look like Robin Williams.

Dr. SACKS. People say now that I'm imitating all his gestures, but it was the other way around.

Senator COHEN. That's all I have, Mr. Chairman. The record will show that during my questioning Dr. Sacks tried very hard to keep his foot still but was not successful.

Senator REID. Senator Pressler.

STATEMENT OF SENATOR LARRY PRESSLER

Senator PRESSLER. Thank you very much. It's a fascinating hearing, and I am here to listen and learn.

I must say that when I first heard of this hearing I was a little bit of a skeptic, but I want to congratulate the staffs and the Senators who thought of it and pulled it together, because it has opened up some new ideas to me.

I, too, saw "Awakenings." I did not read the book, but there was one thing I was fascinated with. I know that the prescription of drugs by psychiatrists is a controversial matter, but, as I understood from the movie—and if this is a real life situation in the book—a certain drug was prescribed, or certain treatment, and the people started to get better, to respond more, and then, after a while, the side effects of the drug brought on some negative characteristics. Is that correct?

Dr. SACKS. Yes. I think to some extent this happens with all drugs, but it was particularly clear and tragic with these patients, probably because there had been so much brain damage. Perhaps 99 percent of the nerve cells which could respond had been knocked out, and a person couldn't maintain normality on the 1 percent remaining. The film actually was somewhat more grim than the reality. In fact, many patients were able to get through some of the side effects and some of them are still alive. One of them, in fact, came along to the set and did a scene.

Certainly, although drugs are not the answer—in Parkinsonism or anything—they were crucial for these patients.

Senator PRESSLER. Well, leading to the Government's role in things such as that—and I had a family member who died of Alzheimer's. I've been fascinated for a long time. There is always a belief by some Alzheimer's patients and their relatives that they can get some drug in Mexico that they can't get here. Our Government, I guess, is fairly reluctant to allow drugs to be used by people until their efficacy and their complete results have been checked out.

Have we been too cautious on letting drugs be tried on people with Alzheimer's, which is hopeless anyway?

Dr. SACKS. That's a delicate question, but I think probably so. We became extremely cautious in this country after the thalidomide tragedy in England and Europe when tens of thousands of people were born with birth defects after mothers had taken the sleeping drug, thalidomide.

I think we are a little over cautious, and certainly with drugs for Parkinsonism and Tourette's syndrome there are many which are very well established and confirmed in Europe but are not available here. Typically people smuggle these in.

I think the situation is less clear with Alzheimer's disease, although there are a number of drugs which are promising for symptoms, and perhaps some others which, at a deeper level, may have some promise of slowing down the disease process, itself.

Senator PRESSLER. Yes.

Now, switching back to the subject of this hearing, music and aging, what are you saying to us as Senators? Should we try to appropriate money to have more music? Should we give NIH money to do research on this? What do you want us to do?

Dr. SACKS. Twenty years ago, when New York State looked into the business of having a music therapist at Beth Abraham Hospital, which is the hospital of "Awakenings," they said, "But this is entertainment. It's trivial. What does it do?"

I showed them the effects of music in our Parkinsonian population and with our Alzheimer's population. I showed them how much the quality of life could be improved and how much all sorts of medical complications could be avoided, and then they changed their minds and they provided funds.

In a practical sense, I think that music therapy and music therapists are crucial and indispensable in institutions for elderly people and among neurologically disabled patients.

I think that what is pragmatic and intuitive needs to be investigated. One needs to know what goes on. There is really no research on the subject. There needs to be research, and there needs to be funding for such research.

I think also there needs to be some proper awareness and respect for music and music therapy so that it is not seen as something just trivial or entertaining.

Senator PRESSLER. Yes; That's an excellent statement.

Now, turning to the NIH—the National Institutes of Health—what does the NIH do that is close to this in terms of research?

Dr. SACKS. I am aware of funding by the National Institute on Aging for research being conducted by Dr. Suzanne Hanser at Stanford University and also by Dr. Kenneth Swartz at the University of Rochester. Dr. Hanser's research is on music therapy with depressed elderly and Alzheimer's patients and their families. Dr. Swartz' research is on musically evoked potentials in the brains of Alzheimer's patients.

Senator PRESSLER. Are there any private research foundations that are doing research along those lines?

Dr. SACKS. Yes. There are certainly some private research foundations. For example, the effects of music with autistic children is a subject of considerable research privately funded. Here special groups like the Parents of Autistic Children are often important in donating funds.

Senator PRESSLER. Thank you very much. I may have some more questions for the record if the record is going to be kept open.

Senator REID. It sure will be. We all have lots of questions for you, Doctor Sacks. We could spend the day with you. Regrettably, we cannot do that. Thank you very much for allowing us to use some of your time here today.

Dr. SACKS. Thank you.

Senator REID. The next panel of witnesses today consists of Mr. Mickey Hart of Sonoma County, CA; and Mr. Theodore Bikel of Wilton, CT.

Would Mr. Bikel and Mr. Hart please come forward?

We will first hear from Mickey Hart.

STATEMENT OF MICKEY HART, SONOMA COUNTY, CA

Mr. HART. Good morning. Thank you for inviting me to speak to you on this issue of great importance to me—the issue of how drumming, the rhythmic manipulation of sound, can be used for health and healing.

I also would like to express my support for the concept of preventative rather than crisis medicine, and specifically the role of music therapy as a means of maintaining mental, spiritual, and physical health in people of all ages.

I am a professional percussionist. For over 40 years I have lived and I have played with rhythm as an entertainer, as an author, and always as a student. Over the last 10 years I have spent much of my time exploring rhythm and its effect on the human body. Why is it so powerful and attractive?

I have written on this subject in my books, "Drumming on the Edge of Magic" and "Planet Drum," which try to address these questions. And yet I know that I have barely scratched the surface, particularly regarding the healing properties of rhythm and music.

Everything that exists in time has a rhythm and a pattern. Our bodies are multidimensional rhythm machines, with everything pulsing in synchrony, from the digesting activity of our intestines to the firing of neurons in the brain.

Within the body, the main beat is laid down by the cardiovascular system, the heart and the lungs. The heart beats between 60 and 80 times per minute, and the lungs fill and empty at about a quarter of that speed, all of which occurs at an unconscious level.

As we age, however, these rhythms can fall out of sync, and then suddenly there is no more important or crucial issue than regaining that lost rhythm.

What is true for our own bodies is true almost everywhere we look. We are embedded within a rhythmic universe. Everywhere we see rhythm, patterns moving through time. It is there in the cycles of the seasons; in the migration of the birds and the animals; and the fruiting and withering of plants; and in the birth, maturation, and death of ourselves.

By acknowledging this fact and acting on it, our potential for preventing illness and maintaining mental, physical, and spiritual wellbeing is far greater.

As a species, we love to play with rhythm. We deal with it every second of our lives, right to the end. When the rhythm stops, so do we. And this is where music becomes important.

According to the late ethnomusicologist, John Blacking, music is a mirror that reflects a culture's deepest social and biological rhythms. It is an externalization of the pulses that remain hidden beneath the business of daily life. Blacking believed that a large part of music's power and pleasure comes from its ability to reconnect us with the deeper rhythms that we are not conscious of, and it is the connection with these rhythms that gives music the power to heal.

Music, as humanly organized sound or vibration, has played a pivotal role in the development of our species, beginning with tool making. The tool record, all those delicately chipped arrowheads and choppers, is a dramatic illustration of our battle to master the subtle body rhythms that any advanced civilization requires to survive.

In order to create the tools that allowed us to move forward as a species, we learned to scrape, strike, rub, shake, and swing in rhythm. From there we gathered in groups to sing our songs, to tell our stories, to dance our dances—all in rhythm.

We found that by gathering together in this way it reinforced our sense of community and family. The natural extension was the use of rhythm, and specifically percussion instruments, in healing ceremonies by traditional and medical practitioners.

As modern technology takes us further and further from our natural rhythms, the use of percussion for healing has greater potential than ever. Today, without thoroughly understanding it, thousands of people across the country have turned to drumming as a form of practice like prayer, meditation, or the martial arts.

It is a practice that is widely acknowledged to help focus attention and to help people break through of the boredom and stress of daily life. More importantly, drumming is a way of approaching and playing with the deeper mysteries of rhythm.

Typically, people gather to drum in drum circles with others from the surrounding community. The drum circle offers equality because there is no head or tail. It includes people of all ages. The main objective is to share rhythm and to get in tune with each other and themselves, to form a group consciousness, to entrain and resonate. By entrainment, I mean that a new voice, a collective voice, emerges from the group as they drum together.

The drummers each bring their own instruments and drum together for about half an hour. Afterwards there is a discussion of issues of importance to the group. The drumming helps to facilitate this discussion because as they drum the group forms a common bond.

From groups of women drummers, the 12-step groups like alcoholic anonymous, to gatherings of men who are part of the ever-growing men's movement, drumming is used to open up channels of communication and foster community and family.

While some drum groups form around a particular issue, others have no agenda whatsoever except to allow the members an opportunity to come together, play their instruments, and share rhythm.

Older Americans are largely unfamiliar with this movement, and yet these are the people who could benefit the most.

The formation of drum circles among the elderly should be an integral part of any music therapy program. There is a large and enthusiastic group of drummers who could be called upon to lead workshops and make instructional videos to be distributed among the older population now isolated in nursing homes and retirement communities.

It would be emphasized that the object is not public performance because when we speak of this type of drumming we are speaking of a deeper realm in which there is no better or no worse, no modern or primitive, no distinctions at all, but rather an almost organic compulsion to translate the emotional fact of being alive into sound, into rhythm, into something you can dance to.

Through drum circles, the aging population could tap into this realm, into these rhythms. The benefits would be wide ranging.

First, there would be immediate reduction in feelings of loneliness and alienation through interaction with each other and heightened contact with the outside world.

While today many older people spend hours each day sitting in front of the television, drumming is an activity which would allow them direct exposure to younger people from the outside community. Whereas verbal communication can often be difficult among the generations and in the sickly, in the drum circle nonverbal communication is the means of relating.

Natural byproducts of this are increased self-esteem and the resulting sense of empowerment, creativity, and enhanced ability to focus the mind, not to mention just plain fun.

This leads to a reduction in stress, while involving the body in a non-jarring, safe form of exercise that invigorates, energizes, and centers.

There is no question of the substantial benefits which could be derived from increased funding for the study and research of music therapy. This funding is critical to explore the most effective ways to utilize the techniques described here by the other speakers. Billions of dollars are spent each year for crisis care, while little energy is spent trying to figure out how to avoid the crisis to begin with. A shift from crisis medicine to preventive medicine needs to occur.

The introduction of drum circles and percussion instruments into the older American population is a new medicine for a new culture. It was a good idea 10,000 years ago, and it is a good idea today.

Thank you.

Senator REID. Mr. Hart, if you remain seated while Mr. Bikel gives his testimony, we have questions for both of you.

Mr. Bikel.

STATEMENT OF THEODORE BIKEL, WILTON, CT

Mr. BIKEL. Thank you.

Mr. Chairman, if you assume that Dr. Sacks was Robin Williams in disguise, I hope that you are not going to assume that the words that are about to emanate from my mouth will really be spoken by Milli-Vanilli. And I'm going to watch my feet, too, while I speak.

Mr. Chairman and members of the Committee, my name is Theodore Bikel. I am a musician, a singer, and actor. I also serve as President of the Associated Actors and Artists of America, the umbrella organization under whose roof you will find all the unions and guilds representing performers in all disciplines, from theatre to opera, to TV, to films and variety.

What expertise I may have personally I derive from a life-long career as a stage actor and as a concert performer and musician. I am also no stranger to the interaction between the arts and government, having served for 5 years as a member of the National Council on the Arts at a time when that body enjoyed a better reputation than it does today—or at least a better image in the public's mind.

I thank you for having invited me to take part in the inquiry.

Mr. Chairman, as a rule, Congressional inquiries are prompted by pragmatic motives, leading directly to the enactment of some measure or another. While this may very well be the case here, too, I am nonetheless heartened by the impression that in the first instance the Committee seeks information—thought leading to more thought.

If, at some time, a utilitarian purpose will emerge and some programs are put into place, so much the better. But we, too, are in need of this interchange of thoughts, for we come looking not for money, but for knowledge.

For far too long have we looked upon the needs of the elderly with a painfully narrow focus. This is a mistake, by the way, we also make when contemplating the needs of the very young.

As a basic premise, I hope we can agree that to view the needs of the aging in terms of physical survival alone makes very little sense. We are slowly beginning to discard the notion that the care of the very young and the very old are to be viewed primarily in terms of the utilitarian aspects of the process, for there is a demonstrated need to build and nurture the mind through aesthetic awareness.

Human beings are in need of music—indeed, of all the arts, as Dr. Oliver Sacks said—not as frills and luxuries, but as a basic necessity. In the last analysis, mere physical survival is meaningless without its cultural corollary.

The question is constantly posed: survival to what purpose? To eat? To sleep? To wake and eat again? Or to see, to touch, to smell, to hear the sounds of music, of laughter, and of grief. To learn and to continue to learn until the last minute. In other words, enrichment—or, if you prefer, fulfillment.

Mr. Chairman, I cannot attest to the healing power of music the way doctors, scientists, or therapists can. I can only claim what years of experience have demonstrated to me many times over—music not only lifts the spirit, but heals the soul. I have even seen it give a physical lift to persons whose very ability to move was close to zero—as has been described here before—and that led to surprisingly successful attempts at foot tapping, and even dancing.

I have, on numerous occasions, performed in senior citizens retirement homes. Many in those audiences were confined to wheelchairs. Some were even brought in on a gurney. The ambulatory residents, too, were not much better off. Their faces showed resignation, apathy, and lethargy. Health care personnel offered apologies to me in advance, fearing what to a performer might seem like an insulting lack of reception. More often than not, these fears turned out to be unfounded and not only was the lethargy gone while the music played, but the effects lingered on for quite a while afterwards.

I submit that this has less to do with how I play and sing, but rather with the kind of music I make. This is a country of immigrants. Many older Americans have roots and antecedents in Europe and elsewhere. Contrary to popular belief, we are not a melting pot, nor should we be. We are a kaleidoscope. In a melting pot everything flows together to form an ill-defined, no-shape, no-color, indistinct mass. In a kaleidoscope everything is clearly delineated, and all contribute to the beauty of the whole.

Many senior citizens may lose strength and vitality, but they do hold on to the memories of their youth. Anything that evokes these memories will put them into a brighter and happier frame of mind. Mr. Chairman, I am multilingual. I sing in 21 languages, 5 of which I speak with fluency. I have been able to play Greek songs to Greeks, French songs to Frenchmen, Spanish songs to Hispanics, and Russian songs to all manner of Eastern Europeans. Most of all I sing and play what my own family tradition has bequeathed to me by way of Jewish music. Thus I have often observed old and infirm persons as the sounds of their ethnic heritage brought them out of a near-catatonic state. They managed to laugh, to sing along, and even to clap to the sounds of their youth.

It seems to me, Mr. Chairman, that, rather than seeking to eliminate multiethnic diversity in this Nation, we should look to its salutary effects and use it constructively in the treatment of older Americans.

I have so far spoken of the effect of music on older people who live in retirement or nursing homes. Despite the fact that these older folk are constantly surrounded by other residents, by health personnel, by social workers, and other staff, their existence is basically a lonely one.

My own mother, who has been in a home for the past 9 years, feels—rightly or wrongly—that she has little in common with the people around her and keeps mostly to herself. Beyond the day-to-day pleasantries, conversation is apt to lead to disagreements, which in older people rankle more deeply than they would with us. I assume that we are younger. It doesn't always hold true.

However, get these people to sit together and listen to music and a bond develops. The shared experience may not last beyond the recital, but while it is there it is real. That brings up the question of what is to be done for older Americans who are not, for whatever reason, confined to nursing homes, who live alone, or with family.

Even living with the family cannot ward off the feeling of loneliness and isolation. Family members have their own agendas, and quality time with grandma or grandpa is a rare occurrence. Shared musical events with a family are even more rare.

Now, could grandpa get as much from the music in the solitude of his room? Do tapes and records furnished to the elderly have the same beneficial effect as a live musical experience? I doubt it.

If it is true that pets are a source of great comfort and healing for the old, then surely toy dogs won't be just as good. No. It is important: one, for the experience to be live; and, two, to have venues where seniors can share the experience. Day care centers for the aged can play a very useful role here. The same van services which pick up seniors for their regular hospital visits might well be used to carry them to recitals or other musical events; but the events have to be planned with a great deal of care.

Now, this brings up the question of who is to coordinate and lead these activities. I am not referring here to people trained in music therapy. As a rule, in nursing homes, retirement villages, and day care centers, these activities are often dumped in the lap of an already overburdened staff person, a nurse, or a social worker. To direct and supervise these activities they go through some rudimentary crash courses in the arts. I submit that we are missing a bet here.

There is a vast pool of underemployed artists in this country, including musicians, dancers, singers. Some of them may, themselves, be close to retirement age. Would it not be far more beneficial to use these people to plan music, to play it, to encourage older people to participate? Not to replace medical personnel or social workers, but to free them for the duties they are properly trained for— which, in any case, keep them fully occupied.

To be sure, not every artist is a born group leader. People have to be trained to do that, as well. But I submit it is far more difficult to teach a nurse some musical knowledge than it is to teach a musician how to reach out to other people or to teach. A training program for artists to work with the elderly would surely benefit the Nation.

In conclusion, I would ask you to contemplate the following:

Some of our basic assumptions about the aged can be reduced to three equations—old age equals poverty, old age equals loneliness, old ages equals infirmity and sickness. Of course, many old people are neither sick nor poor nor lonely, but for those who are there are ways to alleviate the hardship. Above all, there is music.

With some talent, some skill, and a lot of love, we may be able to employ music to enrich the poor, give company to the lonely, and heal the sick.

Thank you.

Senator REID. Mr. Bikel, I'm fascinated with your statement. Being from Nevada, I have observed a significant change in recent years with the playing of tapes and synthesizers and other technologies that eliminate the need for live music in the minds of some people. The new President of the National Musicians' Union is a man from Las Vegas. He has made the point many times that there should be more things for these people to do who have dedicated their lives to music. I think you have pointed us in the right direction.

Someone asked what the purpose of this hearing is. I think the purpose of this hearing is to alert Congress and the American public that music is an inexpensive way to alleviate pain, loneliness, and suffering, and, in effect, to heal people in some instances. So there is going to have to be more work done to focus attention on the fact that music can do a lot of things that people didn't think it could do. In the words of Dr. Sacks, it is not trivial or only for entertainment purposes.

If we can come out of this hearing with nothing more than that, I think we have made a significant contribution to people's good health.

Mr. Hart, how many drums do you have?

Mr. HART. Many. Hundreds.

Senator REID. You are a collector of percussion instruments?

Mr. HART. I am.

Senator REID. And in reading your book, which I just got last night—I haven't read it, but I will do that before the next week passes—you indicate that there are some musical instruments that you have had stored and haven't had a chance to play with them.

Mr. HART. Not many, but a few.

Senator REID. Tell us specifically how you feel drumming or music can be used as preventive health care to keep medicine expenditures down.

Mr. HART. Well, drumming really is the artful manipulation of rhythm and noise. That empowers you. When you hear a loud sound, it allows you to center around it, it describes the sacred space where you are going to play, and it enhances your concentration. It releases adrenalin. It does a lot of things. It allows for community. This is the most important thing. It allows you to share rhythm with someone on an equal basis. I think that's the biggest power of music.

Senator REID. Obviously you and the Grateful Dead have had some indication of what pleases people because you have been going longer than anyone imagined you could. This year you are the leading tour group in the world.

Mr. HART. That's what they say.

Senator REID. Part of that success was your two concerts in Las Vegas, which were two of your biggest.

Mr. HART. Yes. This is what we would call group rapture. This is where a lot of people come together to share an experience, and that's what music is all about, really—to share that experience.

Senator REID. And I think we have all experienced the anticipation of going to someone you really wanted to listen to, and when you get there it is exciting. That's what we are talking about here on a smaller scale, are we not?

Mr. HART. Yes, that's true.

Senator REID. I'd like you both to comment on this. Rhythmic entrainment is a well-established principle in the physical sciences. You put two clocks or a number of clocks in this room, and soon they will tick together. That's a scientifically proven fact.

Can you gentlemen describe in your own words this phenomenon and tell us how this could relate to human health?

Mr. HART. Entrainment isn't just a mechanical law. It also has to do with the heart. You can entrain to a city. You can entrain when you walk down the street with your wife. You can entrain with her. You walk in time with her. You beat in time with someone. That's what entrainment really is. It is the rhythmic resonance that you have with somebody or something around you, and that's what music does, and that's the main ingredient in group music. When you play music privately, that's another story. You entrain with the drum or the instrument you are with. It is a focusing technique.

The drum happens to be one of the most elegant tools that man has ever devised for the making of rhythm, and that's why I believe so strongly in rhythm.

Mr. BIKEL. I have been in many societal situations, Senator, where the togetherness aspect of the music was almost as important, and sometimes more important, than the music, itself. The music was not necessarily well sung or well played, because it is not always played by professionals or by people who devote their life to music, but that togetherness aspect created something that was far greater than the music that was being made.

I recall in the 1960's when I was arrested in the South for civil rights activity and put in jail for a period that the music kept us alive together, and while we were put in segregated jails—the whites in one portion of the jail and the blacks in another—we sang across the courtyard with each other and we were one. It meant more than the music.

Senator REID. You talk a lot about ethnic music having a powerful affect on people from that ethnic group. If we refer back to Dr. Sacks' written testimony there are a couple of lines here that say, "So it is not sufficient usually to put on a loud rock band or Muzak. There must be a sensitive exploration, first of the kind of music that works for each patient. There is no general music. Music is particular and it works in the first place by evoking a particular response."

That's why, when you go to—at least I'm asking if you will agree with me—that's why when you go to a retirement home and, for example, there are people there who are Jewish, and you sing something in Yiddish, that could bring back a memory of that person's childhood; is that right?

Mr. BIKEL. It is absolutely correct, and it really enlivens not only the moment, but brings back a whole slew of associated things that the people had buried somewhere. It brings them out of their shell.

Senator REID. I hope you had the opportunity to listen to the excerpt I read from Dana Gentry, who used to work for me. It is a wonderful story, and I only read part of her letter. This woman's grandmother was in a trance—using the words of Dr. Sacks. She was oblivious to everybody around. She and her mother would go feed this elderly woman because she couldn't feed herself. One day Dana just started singing "True Love," from the musical "High Society." It was something that the grandmother had sang with her grandchild. As soon as she started singing this song, for the first time the grandmother came awake. Now music is what they use for therapy with this woman.

Even though it is for brief periods, the grandmother is herself for a very short period of time.

We appreciate very much your adding your expertise as musicians to the medical testimony rendered by Dr. Sacks.

Mr. BIKEL. I gave a copy of a letter to Dr. Sacks just before this session started which arrived in my home only three days ago. A woman wrote to me after I had given a concert in Saint Louis. It was from a little town in Missouri. She had brought her autistic son, who was 30 years old and deaf because of his autism—deaf to all intents and purposes. He reacts for some reason or another to my music. They have tapes of my stuff playing in the car. They brought him to the concert. She said, as a footnote, he's not even Jewish. And at the end of my concert he stood up and made the love sign in sign language, and on the way home in the car the son turned to his mother and he said, "I hear a bird singing." And that person is deaf.

Senator REID. Senator Cohen.

Senator COHEN. Thank you, Mr. Chairman.

Mr. Hart, is this the first time you have ever testified before a Congressional committee?

Mr. HART. No. I testified in support of the rain forest about 2 years ago.

Senator COHEN. I was going to say I thought it would be entirely appropriate that your first appearance be in the Hart Building. I guess I can't say that now.

Mr. HART. Feels like home.

Senator COHEN. And I was curious, when you stated—by the way, I must say I feel some affinity. One of my sons, who has followed you across the country at least once and back——

Mr. HART. God save you.

Senator COHEN. And I never quite understood what the term "dead head" meant until I listened to the music.

Mr. HART. Excuse me, Senator? Could you clarify that?

Senator COHEN. I meant that in a positive way. He is a big fan, and I have tapes of yours that we both listen to quite frequently.

You mentioned in your book in one of the passages that a village without music is a dead place. That's an African proverb. Is it your assessment that the same applies for the soul? A person without the music is a dead place, as such? Does that apply?

Mr. HART. Well, we have had music in every culture since prehistory. We have seen it on the walls of the caves in 15,000 B.C. We have seen it in the rather godless cultures of 8,000 and 10,000 years ago. We have seen it in every culture worldwide. There must be a reason for this. We couldn't be making this story up.

We find that all cultures have music of some kind—some vocal music, some percussion music. It is inherent to the nature of man. This is just that simple.

We love to dance to our music. We make music to celebrate. We make music to communicate, to be born by, to die by. All rites of passage usually are accompanied by some musical accompaniment.

So I would say without music it would be a dead place. Yes.

Senator COHEN. I noticed you said before that when the music stops we die. I remember that song by Don McLean, "The Day the Music Died." It was a very powerful song.

Mr. HART. I might add something, Senator, that I overlooked before. There are two ways to listen to music. We're not talking about entertainment here. There is a spiritual way. There is a realm of the spirit, which goes to the soul, and then there is the entertainment message. Music is far-reaching. Music therapy is just the latest development in the understanding of vibration. That's really what it is all about—rhythm and vibration.

Senator COHEN. Mr. Bikel, if I were a rich man I would still want very much to hear your music. In fact, it plays over in my mind so many times at various moments—and not when we're talking about Congressional pay raises, I can assure you.

But let me ask you: What do you think the role of the arts community should be in this particular category? You mentioned that perhaps it doesn't hold up to what it used to be in today's times. What is the role of the arts community — and Mr. Hart, as well? Should we be trying to train artists to go into nursing homes, to rest homes, to deal with the elderly? Is there a training program that the arts community ought to be supporting and sponsoring? I know that you have volunteered much of your time in doing this. Do you think that an organized, institutional approach has some merit?

Mr. BIKEL. I advocate it, especially in light of the fact that the profession is so over-crowded. There are too many people chasing too few jobs, and there are many unemployed musicians, unemployed singers, and unemployed dancers who wait on tables, or perhaps just wait for the next job to come along. But they have years of training in music and their talents can be put to good use by training them how to do these things, to work with older people, with sick people, and to have them do good music in the places where the good music is needed.

Senator COHEN. So you think, then, the National Endowment for the Arts ought to be directing some of its energies in this field?

Mr. BIKEL. I think it ought to think along those lines. Yes.

Senator COHEN. Mr. Hart, how about you? In terms of training other individuals to start engaging in music therapy, as such—as you indicated, it is not simply entertainment, it's curative. I was particularly interested in your notions of wellness. You didn't phrase it as wellness, but that's inherent in what you were saying about the importance of music in creating a sense of self esteem, which is vitally important to maintaining a physical wellbeing, as well.

Mr. HART. Yes. Like Mr. Bikel said, there are a lot of unemployed musicians around, and they could be used. This could be a task force kind of a thing. They could go into retirement homes and hospitals, they could lead group drumming circles, they can instruct, they could participate. There is an army out there. They just need the word to march. It's just one of those things. There are a lot of musicians. As a matter of fact, I believe 1 percent of the population we would consider drummers. In this world we figured out that there is about 1 percent of the population that are drummers.

Mr. BIKEL. We have Meals on Wheels, why not have Music on Wheels coming to the homes?

Senator COHEN. Thank you very much.

Mr. Hart, just one curious thing. In your book you referred—one of the chapters I think is Hole in the Sky, and you refer to a Joseph Campell.

Mr. HART. That's correct.

Senator COHEN. Was he the model for the book "The Peaceful Warrior"?

Mr. HART. The model for what?

Senator COHEN. "The Peaceful Warrior." You refer to him as a warrior.

Mr. HART. No. Not really. Joe is a good friend, and he was a warrior in his own right. Anybody can be a warrior. He just happened to discover the power of the drum in his search for the origin mists of our species. We find that most of the origin stories have percussion in them. Joe was an intrepid warrior. He went after it. We shared these interests. There were only a few people that I could talk to about stalactites in 20,000 B.C. He was one of them. So he was a warrior, but no.

Senator COHEN. Thank you very much.

Senator REID. We have a vote pending, so we are going to have to terminate the hearing at this time. We appreciate very much the testimony of Mr. Hart and Mr. Bikel. You have added significantly to this hearing.

What I'd like to do—and this is very unusual, Senator Cohen—while we are gone, which will be about 7 or 8 minutes, is call on Ken Medema to come and entertain the audience while I am not here and while Senator Cohen is not here. This may be one way to employ musicians, because we are gone a lot.

We shall return. The Committee stands in recess for about 10 minutes.

[Recess.]

Senator REID. Ken, thank you very much.

The next panel we will have today is older Americans who remain active performers. First we will have Mr. Jerry Lorance of Muncie, Indiana; and Dr. William Chase of San Clemente, California.

Again, we very much appreciate your patience.

Please proceed, Mr. Lorance.

STATEMENT OF JERRY LORANCE, MUNCIE, IN

Mr. LORANCE. Mr. Chairman, I want to admit one thing here. I never heard of a music therapist in my life. I live so far back in the woods that maybe they haven't reached us. I imagine they have them in Indianapolis, but to my knowledge Muncie has never had a music therapist. I think it is wonderful that there are people like this that are working at this. It is really wonderful.

Music has always meant so much to me. I have played music, one instrument or another, since I was 5 years old—not well, but I played it.

I had a stroke, and I was paralyzed on the right side. My speech was gone. The first thing, and about the only thing, that came in my mind right then was that I'll never play or sing again.

They took me home from the hospital, and I had a small keyboard in the family room. Believe me, that's where I lived. Every chance I got, I went to that keyboard. I had to move that arm. I had to get my fingers to work again.

I finally moved my arm, and I played with my fist doubled up—anything, just to make music. It was everything to me.

I progressed. I could play less than a minute at a time when I started. I finally got up to 45 minutes, and I told my wife, "Hey, I'm going back to work, because 45 minutes is all a musician plays. He can rest 15 minutes." And I did. I have a band—combo. I went over to the place they were playing, and they wanted me to sing with them that night, one song anyway. You know, I did, but I shouldn't have. I never lost out on a beat of the music, but the words—I didn't think those words would come out of my mouth. I was thinking right, but the words were altogether different. It was easier to sing the words, though, than to talk them. The rhythm of it really helped me. It's the only job I ever had in my life that I can be worn out, tired, and go to work, and relax and feel good by the time I get through. It relaxes me.

It is terrific, I think, when you can be a part of music. I play for nursing homes in Alzheimer's wards. What a difference music makes in their lives. You go in and there is no expression. They are sitting there. You start to play, and there is a little light that comes in their eyes. They get up. They dance with each other. They dance around the floor by themselves. It's terrific to see them.

They may not know their name, or where they are from, or who comes to see them, but they know the words to "I Want a Girl," and "When you wore a Tulip," and they'll sing it loud and clear. The attendants work hard with these people to give them a little joy in their life.

I play for hospitals, for the Stroke Club. I look around and see people that there, but for the grace of God, go I. They are paralyzed.

But when you play you can see a little finger moving, or a toe that taps to a rhythm. Music gets through to them.

My wife has been right with me every step of the way. Without her help and understanding I couldn't have made it. But music was so strong in me. I had to come back and play music.

I thought my wife was very strict with me. There was no sympathy that I could find in her. But I found out later that sympathy doesn't work when you are trying to move after a stroke. It is very rewarding for me to play nursing homes and hospitals. You become friends with these people, and they look forward to your coming back and playing for them. Many of them never have a visitor.

I make up song sheets, and they really enjoy singing back in the music of their life. They can remember songs. We'll have a game where I play songs and have them guess them and guess the years they came out, and it is amazing how they know the songs and close to when they came out.

It has been a very rewarding experience for me, and I never knew that people were music therapists. I'm so glad that they are here.

Thank you very much.

[The prepared statement of Mr. Lorance follows:]

TESTIMONY OF JERRY LORANCE FROM MUNCIE, IN

Music has always meant so much to me—I have played one instrument or another since I was 5 years old. When I had a stroke I was paralyzed on my right side and my speech was gone. I thought that I'd never play or sing again.

When they sent me home from the hospital, my keyboard in the family room was my focal point. I had to conquer it—the arm had to move—the fingers had to bend. I had to sing the songs again. It was a very difficult process. I couldn't work at it over a few minutes at a time. Each day I progressed a little further. My arm moved a little more, my fingers bent a little easier, and I could finally put three or four words together instead of the singular words I was able to say. It was easier to sing the words that to talk them.

I finally progressed so that I could play for forty five minutes at one time. That's as long as you have to play at one time before you take a fifteen minute break. I was anxious to get back with my Combo and play again. It was difficult the first few times and the singing didn't always come out the way I thought it would. I didn't lose the beat but some of the words weren't exactly as I had intended, but I was back playing and singing again. It was great!

It's the only job I've ever had where I can go to work tired or worn out and I can relax while I'm playing and feel rested by the time I'm through. I enjoy listening to recorded music but my first love is being able to play and perform live music.

Music is terrific when you can be a part of it. I play for nursing homes and Alzheimer's wards. What a difference music makes in their lives. Most people have very little expression on their faces when I walk in, but when I start playing there's a light in their eyes! Some don't know who they are or where they are but they know the words to "I Want A Girl" or "When You Wore A Tulip" and sing it loud and cheerful. Music awakes something in them, some get up and dance with each other or by themselves. The attendants work hard with these people to give them a little joy in living.

I play for the hospital and also for the Stroke Club. I look around and see those that are less fortunate than I and I think there, but for the grace of God, goes I. I start playing and I see a finger that moves with the music or a toe taps out rhythm. Music gets through!

I was a casket salesman for twenty five years. When I retired I found I had to have an additional income. I turned to music and crafts. It was quite a change of professions I had never cut a piece of wood or painted anything in my life. It was an interesting challenge.

My wife had been right with me every step of the way. Without her help and understanding I couldn't have made it. After the stroke she spent hour upon hour getting me to talk and to get over my paralysis. I thought she was very strict with me at the time but I knew it was for my own good. Sympathy doesn't work when you are trying to recoup from a stroke.

It is very rewarding for me to play for nursing homes. You become friends with the people there and they look forward to the day when you come and play for them again. I make up song sheets and they really enjoy singing the music of their life.

Senator REID. Thank you, Mr. Lorance.

Doctor Chase.

STATEMENT OF WILLIAM CHASE, M.D., SAN CLEMENTE, CA

Dr. CHASE. Well, I'm William Anthony Chase. I've been a doctor for the last 54 years. I am 78 years young.

I have never really heard much about music therapy, but I have been aware of the fact that it is probably the oldest treatment modality on this planet. It begins with the mother giving aid and comfort to her newborn baby. Only women have the capability of making those wonderful clucking, crooning, kind of sounds which get down into the baby and cause the baby to give up screaming and crying and to go to sleep. Men don't have that capability, but women do.

Anyway, frankly, I never heard of music therapy, as this gentleman said just a short while ago, until this whole thing came up before my attention. However, I am a volunteer. I am in active practice of medicine, still, and I also am a volunteer for the Beverly Manor Convalescent Hospital, and also at the Adult Day Health Care Center in San Clemente, CA. There I have had the privilege and the pleasure to have seen with my own eyes exactly what music can do with people who are otherwise almost completely unable to handle themselves physically, emotionally, or mentally.

It is a great pleasure for me to go there, because I know what is going to happen. When I first began, the people would be very listless, lethargic, and very, very withdrawn to the point where they would hardly notice me tuning up my violin. But then, as I would play, they would begin to stamp their feet and to clap their hands and even to sing. The people who were very antisocial among each other, who would never notice the person sitting alongside of them or behind them or in front of them, all of the sudden would interact with their neighbors, which is a very important thing in a convalescent hospital where patients are crowded together.

There is a lot of hostility that can develop if one patient's wheelchair crosses another patient's and maybe snags her foot or something like that. I have noticed that the interpersonal relationship between patients improves very greatly.

I have also noticed the fact that television and radio does not seem to provide the same sort of reaction in these people that live music invariably does. The life which is contained in music which is produced right then and there seems to penetrate into their lives and stimulates them to all kinds of beautiful activity.

I was playing at the Beverly Manor one day, and we were playing a lively song, and all of the sudden a woman who had been wheelchair-bound for years began to stamp her feet and move her fingers and wave her hands, and then suddenly she began to ease up out of the wheelchair and, believe it or not, she arose to her feet and began to tap her feet and dance the shuffle dance in time to the music. The head nurse of the hospital saw that and she rushed up because she was afraid that the patient was going to fall. She grabbed her and she danced along with the patient until the music ended. Now every time I go there this same person greets me with a smile, where before there was nothing—no recognition whatsoever. And she invariably gets up and dances with somebody from the nursing staff.

I have asked the nurses how long this feeling of euphoria lasts after a session of playing like this, and she says generally for at least the rest of the afternoon. And then gradually they creep back into their former selves. It would be very nice if this sort of thing could be provided on a daily basis.

I feel strongly that, with the help of government, there should be some way whereby music therapy can be provided on an almost daily basis to these places where they need it so badly.

I feel very strongly that music therapy is something that is going to pick up momentum and which is going to be a very, very important part of our treatment program—much better than medicine.

[The prepared statement of Dr. Chase follows:]

TESTIMONY OF WILLIAM A. CHASE, M.D.

The musical pharmacopoeia provides for stimulation and for relaxation. As human beings we are introduced almost from the first moments of life to the soothing effects of the musical sounds which seem to be the natural communication between mother and infant. Mothers combine the pleasant sounds of their voices with rocking motions which intensify the feeling of well being in the child allowing it to drift off to sleep. I consider this response to sound and to motion to be the precursor to our appreciation of music which is almost always accompanied by words and by movements.

As we enter childhood we learn to sing and to move in rhythm to music in our classrooms. Music then stimulates a type of social interaction between boys and girls in which the difference between the sexes becomes noticeable, especially to the children themselves so that the groundwork for entry into adolescence is prepared. Adolescence is a stormy period in our lives; we are suddenly confronted by feelings and thoughts which are new and very exciting. Our world is now populated with gorgeous creatures of the opposite sex and music becomes an acceptable excuse to get close to someone and to engage in romantic movements called dancing. Dancing combines with the singing of love songs eventually and eventually leads to marriage and to reenactment of the cycle of life.

Music is a universal force; there is no place on this earth, no matter how primitive, where some sort of musical expression is not used. Each tribe or nationality has developed celebrations which are characterized by uniquely stirring music which stimulates dancing and singing and also, unfortunately, fighting. The Australian aboriginees have their weird sound corroborees accompanied by a form of dancing which is completely foreign to every other society. Indian tribal dances are accompanied by the sounds of tom-toms together with very vigorous chanting. The Scots have their "Highland Flings" which are extremely vigorous dances stimulated by their particular type of music. The Irish have their jigs, the Poles their polkas,

the Russians cossack music, and Hawaiians have combinations of extremely soothing music and dancing of the hulas together with the very vigorous dances pertain-
ing to warfare.

We in this country have had a large variety of dances which are mobile responses
to the stimuli provided by waltzes, fox trots, polkas, swing, jitterbug, and rock and
roll music. Music obviously has been the motivating force for happy interaction between people of all age groups from infancy to senility.

I have noticed in my interactions with older people, many of whom were disabled
to some degree, that music was a unifying force around which they rallied in song
and bodily movements. Older people returned to the days of their youth and in
many instances remember words and music which they sang and danced to in their
youth. It so happens that my period of youth corresponds with those of senior citizens so that I remember many of the old time songs which were popular in those
days. I cannot imagine older people to appreciate many of the current popular
songs, but I can picture these young people when they become seniors to be stimulated by the music of today.

Music has an effect upon all of our emotions. It can make us respond happily, but
it can also impart a feeling of melancholy. One of the most beautiful songs ever
written in my opinion is "Galway Bay"; but it has a melancholy tone to it which is
stirring to the soul and evokes all kinds of emotions in older people. Music is also a
force in the unification of people so that political goals can be reached. The "Mar-
seillaise" with its combination of soul stirring words and music brought about the
collapse of the aristocratic rule in France. The "Battle Hymn of the Republic" con-
tributed to the end of slavery in our country.

Music is very important in the Armed Forces; I remember very clearly in World
War II where as a Battalion surgeon in the 128th Infantry Regiment of the 32nd
Division, I had participated in a 150 mile march over a period of five days with full
combat pack. This was our final training maneuver before we were again thrown
into combat against the Japanese in New Guinea. The purpose of this march was to
acquaint the new troops with the hardships of battle. The new troops were brought
in to fill our ranks which had been very much depleted during our battle against
the Japanese at Buna in New Guinea between September of 1942 and February of
1943.

This march was extremely grueling. We were given very little time for rest. Ra-
tions were skimpy; there was no time for the taking of showers or for shaving. Personal hygiene was minimally achieved. We were a sorry looking lot when we approached the end of our journey at the entrance of Camp Cable just north of Brisbane, Australia. We were bedraggled; we stumbled along. Many of us were in
danger of collapse and then suddenly we heard the spirited playing of "The Campbells Are Coming", our regimental marching music. The regimental band was
spared the rigors of our march and had met us at the camp boundary. Our bedraggled ranks immediately, without any urging from officers, formed up into proper
order. Each platoon in each company formed up in our proper marching position
and we marched into camp with every man's head up, shoulders back, shoulders
squared, every man in perfect step. What was more important, all of us derived the
felling from this experience that no matter what befell us in our encounters with
the enemy we would be able to muster the energy needed to cope with our problems. General Montgomery, the British Commander in North Africa, summed up
the situation very succinctly when asked whether or not he needed more troop rein-
forcements. He responded by saying, "just send me a couple of bagpipers".

My direct participation in the production of music began when I was approximately eight years old. My immigrant parents were extremely ambitious for all of
their children, and especially me since I was the only boy in the family and I was
urged to take violin lessons which were provided me by a Czechoslovian teacher by
the name of Ottokar Vyszehrad. My teacher was a very fine violinist but unfortunately he did not become aware of the fact that I really did not know how to read
music. He never really taught me anything about keys or positions or anything of
that sort. He would place a sheet of music on the stand and then play it, and I
would play it right back at him. He undoubtedly thought that I could read music.
After several years he told my parents that I needed to have a more accomplished
teacher because I was apparently too good for him and so he sent me to a teacher
by the name of Adam Kurillo in the Metropolitan Opera House fairly close by to
where we were living on the lower east side of New York.

I presented myself to Mr. Kurillo's studio and he placed a bit of music on a stand
and said, "play it", and I looked at the notes and I could not really read what the
notes said and I let him know that he became enraged and smacked me over my
back with his bow and yelled out, "zaba", which in Polish means 'toad'. I picked up

my violin, packed it away, and left the studio and never went back. I never took any more lessons after that. However, I kept on playing for people who visited my home and I also played at Christmas eve and at family gatherings and people seemed to like it.

If I heard a song I could generally play it fairly well, and it still persists to this day; I have not taken up a serious study of music, but I am able to pick up the melodies of most pieces if they are not too complicated. I am, then, by no means a virtuoso, but people seem to like my music and that's what counts; at least it counts when I play for older people who have no way of escaping from my violin playing. Actually they seem to like it to the point where they keep on asking for me to play more and more all of the time. It is a thrill to me that I am able to communicate some sort of pleasure to old people who would otherwise have nothing very pleasant to look forward to from time to time.

I made it. a tradition to play Christmas Carols around the neighborhood every year, except when the weather is too bad, and people look forward to Christmas eve and come over to my house. We start out from there and make the rounds of our entire neighborhood with people coming out greeting us and singing along with us and joining up with us as we go. It is a tradition now where I live in California and it was also a tradition in New York when we lived there.

During the time of World War II I was able to buy a very inexpensive fiddle in Brisbane, Australia, and take it with me to New Guinea where I was known as 'the crazy American doctor who played the fiddle on the front lines'.

I make music with my violin to the patients at the Beverly Manor Convalescence Hospital in Capistrano Beach, California, and also to the Adult Day-Care Center. The patients in these facilities seem to accept me very enthusiastically so that it has become a custom for me to play at both facilities weekly.

People await me with much anticipation and they greet me with obvious enthusiasm and joy and during my performances they clap, they wave their hands, they stamp their feet, they sing, and in general express much happiness and awareness of the presence of stimulating music.

I prefer to play the happy songs from the 20s, 30s, and early 40s and I, of course, do not play any rock and roll type of music because this is completely foreign to them. The kinds of songs that were popular during the post World War I era are extremely tuneful and stimulating and I have no doubt that the people who appreciated that music in the early days retained memories of it and also the playing of that music reawakened memories within themselves of their happiest days of their youth.

Particularly I must say that my accompanist is a very charming lady who is somewhat afflicted with the loss of recent memory and she is able to, after I have played several bars of music, jump right in with her piano and accompany me to the very end and on all of these, even the complicated songs, and perform extremely well. Her memory is such that she does not remember how she gets to the place where she is performing and her husband must keep track of their dates and must bring her there personally. All it takes is my playing several notes and she is right there with me and we go right to the very end and people just appreciate it and love it and love her and I certainly think extremely highly of her capabilities. I know that these songs are down deep in her soul and they are an integral part of her existence. No matter what takes place in her life she will always have it with her; she will always be able to do it unless she suffers some debilitating stroke-like condition.

This same situation applies to all of the people in these age groups who respond so enthusiastically and with much movement and song expressing great joy. As far as I am concerned, these songs even though I hear them very seldom I am able to remember and to give a fairly creditable performance upon my violin.

These songs are deeply ingrained within my heart and soul. Music has had a very great influence upon me throughout my entire life. I have always responded appropriately to the mood of the music as I heard it. I am sometimes moved to tears, and sometimes my soul just soars way out into space there with the beauty and movement and thrill of music.

Music also has given me courage to face possible dangers as I stated previously, that the 150 mile forced march was a real test of endurance despite the fact that I had a herniated disk; I was working against the herniated disk which practically crippled me. I kept on and walked every step of the way and was proud of having been able to do so, especially when the end came and we were met by that band playing "The Campbells Are Coming".

Several years ago I developed Dupuytren's contractures which is a condition where the fingers of the hand are placed into extreme flexion by reason of fibrosis involving the tendons and tendon sheaths. Had I not been involved with the playing of the violin I would have probably avoided surgery, but since I was doing so and since my left hand is the hand which determines my fingering on the violin it was absolutely necessary to face surgery which I did twice. Now my fingers, even though there are many scars on my hands, my fingers are able to move fairly nimble across by finger board.

I feel sometimes disappointed in my life because it was obvious to all who heard me when I was a small child that I had a great capability for playing the violin. But as circumstances dictated and as I described, my teacher had not taught me how to read music; also my traumatic experience with the teacher at the Metropolitan Opera House all blended together to take me out of the didactic study of music and give me a chance to become a doctor.

It is a source of wonder to me how I was able to, in the end years of my life, to bring music and medicine together so perfectly by being involved with bringing joy and happiness and good feeling to older people both ways. I very often take my medical bag with me and take care of older people right after I finish playing. I think that God has been extremely good to me and I am thankful that things have turned out the way that they have. I am also thankful to have made the acquaintance of my piano playing partner who exemplifies to me the healing power of music upon the body and soul. I feel strongly that the good Lord has brought us together and has made happier and better people out of us.

Adult Day Health Care Center
of South Orange County
2021 Calle Frontera
San Clemente, California 92672
(714) 498-7671

July 22, 1991

William A. Chase, M.D.
2414 Calle Monte Carla
San Clemente, CA 92672

Re: Special Committee on Aging Senate Hearing
    Forever Young: Music and Aging

Dear Dr. Chase:

I appreciate your asking me to send a letter about the elderly participants of the Adult Day Health Care Center of South Orange County and their reactions to the special music experiences you share with us each week.

As you know, adult Day Health Care Center is a day health care program for older adults who come here on weekdays in order to socialize with their peers, share meals, and actively participate in group events while at the same time having access to the services of health care professionals such as physical therapists, music therapist, occupational therapist, speech pathologists, an audiologist, counseling and nursing staff.

A weekly average of 50 participants come to the center between 8:30 a.m. and 4:30 p.m. Most of the participants have impaired physical and mental functioning due to conditions such as Lupas, Parkinson's Disease, Alzheimers, Addisons Disease, dementia, manic depression, schizophrenia, cancer, emphysema, heart disease and stroke.

The staff and participants all look forward to your special music on Monday Mornings from 10 to 11 a.m. Your lively personality and violin renditions of old favorites really livens up our mornings and gets the week off to a good start.

Mrs. E, your piano accompanist, plays beautifully in spite of some limitations in her short term memory. The participants all sing, smile, tap their feet, clap hands and sometimes even dance while you share your musical talents with us. Many of these people respond only in a limited way to other activities. The music which Mrs. E plays is played from her memory of the music which she studied so long ago. She told me that her formal training was at the Los Angeles Conservatory of Music at the age of 18.

Page 2--William A. Chase, M.D.

Mrs. G., who has had a gastrostomy, usually sits hunched over because of the pain of her osteoporosis. During music, she brightens up and seems to become a different person. She no longer complains and talks of bad dreams, but rather smiles, sits up, and interacts with other people. I really enjoy hearing her sing "In The Garden" in the microphone while you and Mrs. E. play.

Mrs. C., who often sits limp in an almost catatonic state, sings, taps her feet and claps her hands when she hears music. That active participation continues during our music exercise class later in the morning.

We have stroke patients who have very limited verbal skills ("yea, yea, yea" and "no, no, no") who sing songs, initiate some conversation, and seem to really enjoy your music.

After your Monday morning music sessions, the lively, celebrative mood you facilitate with music lasts through the exercise group and mealtime. The smiles, participation, and active, vital interest displayed by everyone are indicative of the value of your taking time each week to share your music talents.

As a physician and musician, you are no doubt aware of the effects of music on a person's physical and mental well-being. Lois Johnson, a 78 year old volunteer who comes every Tuesday morning to play the piano for a "piano bar" for our participants, suffers greatly from arthritis in her back and hands. She tells me that playing the piano helps loosen up her swollen joints and actually helps the arthritic pain decrease.

I am pleased to hear that you have been invited to speak at the Senate Special Committee on Aging Hearing on August 1. It is certainly an historic moment to have the Senate recognize the significant and unique benefits of music therapy for the elderly as well as for other populations. Your thoughts and expertise as a physician and a musician will no doubt be valuable testimony.

Sincerely yours,

JoAnn Bishop, RMT
Activity Director

JB

**Adult Day Health Care Center
of South Orange County**

2021 Calle Frontera
San Clemente, California 92672
(714) 498-7671

July 22, 1991

Dr. William Chase
2412 Calle Monte Carlo
San Clemente, CA   92672

Re: Forever Young: Music and Aging
     Senate Special Committee on Aging
     August 1, 1991

Dear Dr. Chase:

    May we extend our congratulations to you for the
national recognition you have received for your music
therapy by way of the Senate invitation to address the
special hearing on Music and Aging.

    Over the years, our staff has observed and
documented the therapeutic benefits of music in our
program. Many of the participants who are not able to
speak or remember can spontaneously sing and participate
in an activity that is mentally stimulating, emotionally
stirring and spiritually comforting.

    We see the difference music can make in the
participants' well-being and certainly lend our support
to the profession of music therapy and its place in the
health care setting.

Sincerely,

Carol Quintana
Program Director

Marilyn Ditty
Administrator

CQ/sh

"Dedicated To Caring"

TO WHOM IT MAY CONCERN: July 10, 1991

    I am writing to share with you the Spirit of Volunterism combined
with the gift of music. Dr. William Chase one of the many physicians who
currently attend to our Residents at Beverly Manor Convalescent Hospital
in capisttano Beach California. He is also a chair person on our Utilization
Review Committee.

    The difference is in the volunteering spirit. Every Thursday Doctor
Chase's violin act is warmly received by the 45-50 elders of whom all are
wheelchair-bound. The music is uplifting for the residents and there
really is a difference between "Live" music and music from a tape or radio,
our residents react to the movement and the stimulation of their senses.
Doctor Chase walks around and reaches out to touch hands as he brings smiles
to the faces of our residents while playing old favorites on his violin.
It is plain to see the healing power of music, when we as staff watch
victims of strokes, residents with severe depression and residents with
Alzheimer's suddenly perk-up and their eyes sparkle and hands and feet
tap to the tunes.

    As one of our 83 year old female residents so rightly stated; "He sure
knows how to bring back the good old days with his songs, we feel so good,
it makes me think about the times when I could walk and dance".

    We at Beverly Manor Convalescent Hospital certainly have no scientific
evidence of the fact that music is a healing art - but in our small corner
of the world - music is a visible healer every Thursday afternoon.

                        Sincerely,

                        KERRY D. DAVIS
                        Administrator

MUSIC THERAPY REPORT

INTRODUCTION: Music therapy directly contributes to the individuals
                    social, mental, and emotional needs.

                    The focus of concern is peer interaction and participation,
                    the ability to receive information and express language
                    symbols, communication, the ability to use the physical
                    body as a mode of expression, and the opportunity to gain
                    competence in a variety of social roles such as, the giver,
                    receiver, leader.

CASE HISTORY #1

AGE: 83

DIAGNOSIS: S/P CVA

MENTAL STATUS: Fair - unable to verbalize needs secondary to diagnosis.

BACKGROUND HISTORY: Caucasian female, she was treated for CHF. Aphasic
                    due to CVA, has a daughter Nancy. Date of current
                    admission is 1/21/91. Religion is methodist, she
                    attends church at facility.

PAST INTERESTS: She played the violin very well, was part of an orchestra,
                    loves music, other activities include dancing, arts and
                    crafts, table games.

RESPONSE: Resident response has been very good, she smiles, laughs, she
                    gets up out of her wheelchair and starts dancing, she is active
                    while participating, she enjoys the music and peer interaction,
                    she sings along humming to her tunes.

CASE HISTORY #2

AGE: 93

DIAGNOSIS: G.I. Bleeding, Alzheimers

MENTAL STATUS: Alert, oriented to person only, very confused.

BEVERLY
ENTERPRISES

BACKGROUND HISTORY: Caucasian female, date of current admission is 6/4/86. Religion is methodist, she attends services at the facility. Louise was born in Washington, she is a widowed mother.

PAST INTERESTS: Include taking care of her family, sewing, music, gardening.

RESPONSE: Resident response has been positive, enjoyable, relaxing, happy, she sings along, smiles, talks about the good old days. Slaps her hands up against her thighs and clapping her hands as the music plays.

CASE HISTORY #3
AGE, 96
DIAGNOSIS: Senile Dementia

MENTAL STATUS: Very confused and disoriented, unable to answer questions appropriately.

BACKGROUND HISTORY: History was obtained from daughter, she was born in Sicily, came to the United States in 1910. Resided in New York. She was married for 60 years and is now widowed. Has four daughters.

PAST INTERESTS: She was very active in catholic church and Italian Societies while she lived in New York, worked during WW II as supervisor in a plant. Later was a garment worker in a factory. Likes music very much.

RESPONSE: Resident response has been very good. She sings along with the music, fully participating, clapping hands, showing sings of enjoyment, happy and stimulated. Resident who never responded to stimuli prior - now claps her hands and sings along very loudly.

CASE HISTORY #4

DIAGNOSIS: Zenker's Diverticulum and cricopharyngal muscle spasm, also severe dysphagia secondary.

AGE: 85

MENTAL STATUS: Alert and oriented, mentally sound, can speak clearly, and can answer questions correctly.

BACKGORUND HISTORY: Female resident was admitted 4/23/91, religion is Jewish. She was born in New York, lived their for years, never had any children, but was married and now is widowed.

PAST INTERESTS: Include teaching, reading, music, travel.

RESPONSE: Resident response is very encouraging and positive. She participates in an active manner by singing the words, smiling at times and laughing out loud, it is evident she enjoys herself very much. This resident rarely participates in any activities but always comes to this musical hour.

CASE HISTORY #5
AGE, 85
DIAGNOSIS: Cerebrovascular Accident, dementia, history of sepsis, urinary tract infection and gastrointestinal bleeding.

MENTAL STATUS: Alert, disoriented, excessive yelling. Can speck clearly.

BACKGROUND HISTORY: Resident caucasian female, admitted on 2/23/88, was born in California and lived in San Juan Capistrano for many years.

PAST INTERESTS: Resident attended business college and enjoyed school, later became a secretary working in insurance field. She was president of many social clubs and groups. Resident enjoyed music, reading and social clubs.

RESPONSE: Resident response is very good. She starts singing the words and clapping her hands, she just about jumps out of her chair, enjoys the event very much, and is not disruptive during the program at all. she becomes very appropriate in her interactions.

Senator REID. Dr. Chase, I'm wondering if you could relate to Senator Cohen and me the woman that accompanies you. Would you tell us about her?

Dr. CHASE. Yes. She is 70 years old, and she has short-term memory loss. I don't want to put a name on that, but I think you all know what I mean.

Senator COHEN. That's 70 years young.

Dr. CHASE. Well, she's 70 years young. But when she plays the piano, there is no hesitation about what she is going to do there. I never tell her what I'm going to play. I just start playing, and within two bars she has the melody, which she dredges up from way down deep in her soul, and she plays the thing faultlessly with me. The people just love it.

Senator REID. You play the violin and she plays the piano?

Dr. CHASE. I play the violin and she plays the piano. That's right.

Senator REID. How did you discover she could do this?

Dr. CHASE. Frankly, I don't know. One day I happened to be there making rounds at the Beverly Manor Convalescent Hospital and I heard her play. I said, "Gee, she sounds like a very good possible accompanist for me." We got together and, surely enough, we hit it off immediately.

Senator REID. Can you converse with her when she is not playing the piano?

Dr. CHASE. Yes, except that her memory loss is very, very sad. We were invited to play at the Presbyterian Church there, and I accepted the invitation. Her husband was unable to take her there, so I picked her up and drove her there. We played, and at the end of the program she approached my wife and said, "I don't know how I got here. How am I going to get home?" I drove her down there, and she had no memory of my having done so.

So Alzheimer's is a very sad thing; however, she was able to dredge up all these beautiful songs from way back. We never discuss what we are going to play. I'll just start something and she comes right along with it—especially the more cheerful songs. The lively songs are important to her, and also to the people who listen.

Senator REID. I appreciate that.

Mr. Lorance, what musical instrument do you play?

Mr. LORANCE. I play keyboard now. I played saxophone and clarinet for about 30 years.

Senator REID. And you said that after you had your stroke and when you were in the recovery process, when you were paralyzed on the right side, you had an urge to play music?

Mr. LORANCE. Oh, yes.

Senator REID. And when you first started playing did you try the keyboard? Is that what you worked on?

Mr. LORANCE. Yes.

Senator REID. And you said you couldn't play with your fingers; is that right?

Mr. LORANCE. Yes. They wouldn't bend. I couldn't open my hand. I finally got my arm to move so I could put my hand up on the keyboard, and I know it doesn't sound too good, but it's better than nothing. I just rolled the hand on the keys, and you can make music. You can make music anywhere.

Senator REID. And you feel without any question that the therapy that you conducted on yourself has led to your recovery?

Mr. LORANCE. Yes.

Senator REID. No doubt about that?

Mr. LORANCE. No.

Senator REID. Senator Cohen?

Senator COHEN. Dr. Chase, based on your experience with the residents at the center, would you see these musical sessions as activity that enhances the quality of life of the residents, or medical therapy, or both?

Dr. CHASE. I have no question. Absolutely. Yes, both.

Senator COHEN. So it would be both enhancement of quality of life and medical therapy?

Dr. CHASE. Yes.

Senator COHEN. Is it as effective, from what you have observed, as speech therapy? Do you have the same kind of results when you have a speech therapist go in, or is it more effective?

Dr. CHASE. Well, I feel that at the moment of subjecting the patient to music therapy the results are very impressive and they are immediately discernable. I don't know of any medicine that is of any particular benefit in Alzheimer's. If you have disturbed patients, you have them under sedation, which only intensifies the problem there because people tend to become sensitized and to become habituated.

Senator COHEN. How long have you been playing the violin?

Dr. CHASE. I began when I was about 7 years of age. I had a teacher who was a very fine violinist, but he did not teach me how to even read music. He put up some music and he would play it, and I would play it back at him, and he thought I knew what I was doing.

Senator COHEN. But, in addition to your profession as a doctor, I assume that you have played over the years for groups?

Dr. CHASE. I have played over the years Christmas caroling on Christmas Eve. The whole neighborhood comes out and follows me.

Senator COHEN. I was somewhat surprised when you said you didn't realize the therapeutic effect of music, having been a lifelong musician.

Dr. CHASE. I only played at family gatherings and Christmas and events like that. I never tried to attach any medical connotation to it. I did buy a fiddle in Brisbane, Australia, and I took it to New Guinea during the campaign—places you never heard of, battles you never heard of. I was known there as the crazy American doctor who played the violin on the front lines. But it wasn't true. I never took the violin to the front lines. I played the violin in the rear areas.

Senator COHEN. Thank you very much. It has been very helpful.

Senator REID. We appreciate very much your patience and, most of all, your testimony. It has been enlightening. We look forward to working with you in the years to come.

The final panel today will be experts in music and health. We will hear from Dr. Alicia Ann Clair, Dr. Frank Wilson, and Dr. Matthew Lee. Dr. Clair is from Topeka, KS; Dr. Wilson is from Danville, CA; and Dr. Lee is from New York City.

We will first hear from Alicia Ann Clair. Please proceed.

STATEMENT OF DR. ALICIA ANN CLAIR, TOPEKA, KS

Dr. CLAIR. I want to thank you for the opportunity to speak with you today to increase awareness of music therapy as a valid and efficacious treatment and health care service for older Americans. I am the Director of Music Therapy at the University of Kansas in Lawrence, KS, and a research associate at the Colmery-O'Neil Veterans Affairs Medical Center in Topeka, KS. Both these institutions are very long supporters of music therapy, but I speak not as a representative of either of those institutions today, but as a long-time practicing professional music therapist who has been working with and conducting research with elderly Americans since 1977.

I began my clinical music therapy work with well elderly persons in developing and redeveloping their music skills to give them opportunities to demonstrate their abilities and competencies to succeed musically. Some of these people included people such as Narcissus Abella, who was a World War II veteran who survived the Bataan Death March and who learned to play the clarinet when he was 82 years old—something that he said he always wanted to do.

Evangeline, a widow who lived in a farmhouse 15 miles from town—very isolated—learned to play the guitar in her early 70's, and said she used it to play away her blues and to play when she was happy. She said it didn't really matter how it sounded because it was just the dog and her anyway, and it didn't matter what he thought.

This lady later developed breast cancer. She had surgery. She had follow-up chemotherapy. The music therapy group was very supportive of her during that time. That also helped to motivate her to get back into her social contacts, and she came back to join us again.

I also did music therapy programming with the frail elderly in residential care homes. Here were people such as Grace and Ann, who both had strokes. They could play an autoharp together, but could not play individually. There were others who seemed too depressed to socialize, but they sang when the music therapist conducted sessions. And they all danced in their own way.

More recently I have conducted music therapy sessions with persons diagnosed with dementia and with their families. Music therapy has provided opportunities for social integration with people who have really lost touch and who have become severely dysfunctional to bring them into the here and now. It seems to provide a time out from the terrors and the confusion that they suffer in dementia. It also gives families an opportunity to maintain contact with their loved ones far into the late stages of the disease. Spouses have played music with one another, they have danced, they have drummed together.

Lately Marie, the wife of Bill, after dancing for the first time with him in music therapy, said, "He held me in his arms. It is the first time in years that he has just held me."

I have a short videotape with me today that shows the powerful effects of music in one of the patients with whom we have worked who was severely regressed and confused.

[Videotape presentation.]

48

Dr. CLAIR. In conclusion, my clinical perceptions and research conclusions support the need for legislation and regulation that influences the availability of music therapy services to older Americans and to other populations. It also supports the possibility of using Federal funds to conduct research projects that include demonstration projects, basic research, and clinical outcome research. A modest amount of Federal funds could be extremely helpful and have a major impact on the physical and mental wellbeing of a growing population of older Americans.

Thank you.

[The prepared statement of Dr. Clair follows:]

National Association for Music Therapy, Inc.

8455 COLESVILLE ROAD   SILVER SPRING, MD 20910   (301) 589-3300   FAX (301) 589-5175

EXPERT WITNESS TESTIMONY

Therapeutic Uses of Music in the Elderly

August 1, 1991

Alicia Ann Clair, Ph.D.
Registered Music Therapist-Board Certified
Research Associate
Colmery O'Neil Veterans Affairs Medical Center (11-K)
2200 Gage Blvd.
Topeka, Kansas 66622
(913) 272-3111 X-266

Professor
Director of Music Therapy
Art and Music Education and Music Therapy Department
311 Bailey Hall
The University of Kansas
Lawrence, Kansas 66045
(913) 864-4784

1

EXECUTIVE SUMMARY

I give this testimony as a professional who has practiced music therapy with older Americans since 1977 and as a past President of the National Association of Music Therapy, Inc. I do not speak for the University of Kansas where I am a Professor and Director of Music Therapy, or for the Colmery-O'Neil Veterans Affairs Medical Center in Topeka, Kansas where I serve as a research associate.

I. Therapeutic uses of music have a long history.
    A. The music therapy profession began in the U.S. in Veterans Administration Hospitals in the 1940's to rehabilitate WW II American soldiers.
    B. Research shows music therapy is effective in physical, emotional and social rehabilitation.

II. Music Therapy with the older Americans is relatively new.
    A. As persons age there is a need for interventions which contribute to life quality.
    B. Most older persons like music and like to be involved in it in some way.
    C. The characteristics of music make it viable to use in a broad array of ways.
    D. Music can be designed to promote successful experiences even in those with no prior experiences.
    E. Music can bring people together for common good; e. g. for social contact, emotional support, physical exercise and activity, mutual sharing and others.

III. Music Therapy with well, elderly Americans is innovative.
    A. Elderly persons have the abilities to learn new musical skills very late into life.
    B. These persons have demonstrated these abilities through musical development.
    C. Music therapy programs for well elderly persons can be preventive.
        1. Programs contribute to reminiscence and life satisfaction.
        2. Programs contribute to life quality.
        3. Programs are motivating and stimulating.

IV. Music Therapy with chronically ill older Americans at home is in development.
    A. Music therapy can serve to integrate the family members.
    B. Music can be a form of expression and communication.
    C. Music activities can be adjusted to facilitate success for persons who are very frail.
    D. Music can provide relief from chronic pain.
    E. Music can help people grieve.

V. Music Therapy with frail, elderly American care home residents is ever growing.
    A. Research shows these persons retain their musical abilities to learn.
    B. Music therapists must design programs these persons can manage physically, socially and psychologically.
    C. Music therapy helps to manage stress, insomnia, depression and isolation.
    D. Music stimulates social interaction, sensory awareness and intellectual activities.
    E. Music contributes to life quality and personal dignity.

VI. Music Therapy is very effective with persons who have dementia and their families.
    A. Interventions are direly needed in persons afflicted and their families.
        1. Over one-half of the residents in care homes have dementia of the Alzheimer's type.
        2. Prior to institutionalization these persons' lives and their families are devastated emtionally, socially, psychologically and financially.
        3. Caregivers lose their health and their life quality in the care process
        4. Lives of those afflicted and their caregivers will continually decline--there is no cure.
    B. Music Therapy practice protocols have been developed.
        1. These are successful with those from early through late stages of dementia.
        2. These are designed to incorporate family caregivers into them.

3. These can be used to train family caregivers to use music with their loved one afflicted with dementia, including dementia of the Alzheimer's type.
C. Music Therapy is greatly appreciated by caregivers and families desperate for interventions.
   1. Music Therapy provides ways for families and their afflicted ones to interact socially and emotionally.
      a. Caregivers and families can no longer reach their loved one any other way.
      b. Caregivers have uncertainties concerning how they fit/belong with a parent, sibling or spouse who can no longer communicate verbally with them.
   2. Music Therapy contributes greatly to life quality for caregivers, families and their loved ones afflicted with dementias.
D. Research shows Music Therapy is effective with severely regressed persons with dementia.
   1. Music taps the residual skills and abilities no longer accessible through other interventions.
      a. Caregivers say that the "real" person comes out through music and they get glimpses of the way their loved ones used to be.
      b. Persons with dementias can excercise skills learned well in the past.
      c. Persons with dementias can interact rhythmically until the very last.
   2. Through music persons with dementias can play rhythmically and dance, though singing discontinues as the disease progresses.
      a. When dancing, caregivers can be held by their afflicted loved one, something which contributes to the intimacy in their relationship.
      b. Persons with dementias are drawn to music activities which facilitates engaging them in the activities.
   3. Music stimulates attention and persons with dementias can participate for as long as 30 minutes at a time even in late stages.
   4. Music provides opportunities to interact with others socially, something severely regressed persons no longer can do.
   5. Through music activities, persons with dementias watch one another and indicate their awareness of others, something they do not do in other contexts.
   6. Music provides contact with the here and now, and persons with dementias seem more alert during and following music therapy sessions.
   7. Through music, persons with dementia can organize their responses and even learn new musical behaviors.
      a. This occurs until the late stages of the disease.
      b. Eventually this ability is lost.
      c. To the last hours of life, persons with dementia open their eyes and turn their heads to locate the sound source of music.
VII. Music Therapy is important for caregivers.
A. The terrible devastations suffered when one has a loved one with dementia lead to ill health.
B. Life satisfaction and life quality are destroyed.
C. Caregivers need options for self-care including relaxation and stress management through music.
D. Caregivers need ways to maintain relationships with their loved ones for as long as possible and music therapy can provide them.

THERAPEUTIC USES OF MUSIC WITH THE ELDERLY

Therapeutic uses of music throughout the life span have been incorporated into treatment since the beginning of recorded history. There was reference to them in ancient Greek literature, the Bible and other sources. Though not much is known of specific applications in those early times, a book written in the English language in the mid-1600's and finally published in 1729, presented the use of music as a therapeutic intervention (Gibbons & Heller, 1985). Its author discussed the use of music as therapy to 1) change and evoke moods, 2) trigger memories associated with the music, 3) influence and change physiological processes, and to 4) stimulate and sedate. This treatise was explicit about using music for persons even if they had no prior musical training or experience, and it stipulated designing the music to suit the needs of the individual person. This information is quite astounding when put in its historic perspective. At the time it was published in London, England, Handel had already lived in the city for 17 years, but he had not yet written the Messiah. Yet, these therapeutic uses of music are incorporated into music therapy practice today.

Literature indicates music has been used therapeutically in the United States since the turn of the century, and before. Music therapy began as a profession, however, in the Veterans Administration hospitals in the 1940's where it was incorporated into rehabilitation programs for American soldiers returning from World War II. By 1950 the National Association for Music Therapy, Inc. was established and colleges and universities across the country began offering degree programs to educate and train professional music therapists.

The contemporary definition of music therapy, in its rather broad sense, is the therapeutic use of music to change behaviors. This use depends on careful assessments of individual consumer's therapeutic needs and their musical tastes and preferences. It is also based on the principles of musical influences on physiological, social and emotional behaviors. With these considerations music therapists use their expertise to design, implement and continually evaluate programs for individuals. These programs may include individual or group sessions or a combination of these. They usually also include learning therapeutic music skills to use away from the music therapy session so that independence, and self care is developed. But, whatever the design of the music therapy program, the ultimate goal is to meet the needs of the individual consumer in the most effective, and efficient way and to promote and maintain that consumer's quality of life.

Some Principles of Music Therapy

Pervasiveness of Music

Persons of all ages generally experience music frequently in their lives, many on a daily basis. Many persons use music to relax and some persons have such frequent uses of music that they listen to it virtually all day. Music is almost always used in the celebrations and rituals associated with important life events; i.e., birthdays, anniversaries, weddings, funerals and others. Music is also used to the set the environment for offices, work areas and to influence the mood of special occasions. With the other important uses of music, it is often a part of entertainment and is used to structure leisure time.

The frequent uses of music have led many to refer to music as a universal phenomenon. While some musical elements, such as rhythm, tempo timbre, and others, are universally found, the types of music perferred, understood and used are not the same for all persons in all cultures. There are even differences in the same culture when preferences of the old and the young are compared. The types of music within a community or even within a family from that community may vary according to individuals' ages, backgrounds and experiences. Therefore, music is universal but it is not a universal language.

Music Preference

Music which is preferred and most often used by individuals is the music which is integrated into their lives. This music could be that which was popular during their young adult years (Gibbons, 1977), that which was used in religious services and patriotic ceremonies and that which was used in other cultural and community contexts. Music which is not integrated into an individual's life may simply have no effect or may even be offensive resulting in inattention and disengagement. It is the preferred music which is most likely to stimulate cooperative responses in all persons.

The type or types of preferred music may be determined by interviewing persons, or their family members if they can no longer express themselves verbally. If interview responses are inconclusive or unavailable, it is possible to determine music preferences by using various types of music and observing reactions. Facial expressions, body postures, vocalizations and other overt responses to particular music will show either pleasure or discomfort associated with it. From these overt behaviors conclusions concerning preferences can be drawn.

Purposes for Using Music with the Elderly

Physical and Emotional Stimulation. Music can be used with elderly persons to evoke a wide range of responses. Depending upon how it is structured, music can be sedative to promote relaxation and calm or it can be stimulative to promote movement to other physical activity.

The research literature indicates clearly that the definitions of sedative and stimulative music are individualized and there is no consistent agreement among listeners. What may be calming and quieting to one person may be disturbing and disquieting to another. Individuals with whom the music is used must determine its sedative and stimulative effects.

The sedative and stimulative qualities of music not only evoke calmness or activity, they also evoke other physical responses. Research with subjects in a wide range of ages has shown that music can affect blood pressure, heart rate, respiration, galvanic skin response, pupil dilation, discomfort and/or pain tolerance (Standley, 1986). These reactions to music differ from individual to individual, but there is no question that music is a powerful influence over physiological responses. It may be these physical reactions that are the bases for quieting and active responses to sedative and stimulative music.

These physiological responses to music may also be integral to emotional responses to music, But, whatever the reason, music influences moods and emotions, and there is a large body of literature which supports this fact. A particular emotion can be triggered by certain music for a certain individual and these emotional reactions to specific music seem relatively consistent for that individual. These emotional reactions for persons who are disabled and who cannot communicate verbally can be unpredictable and are, therefore, discovered by chance unless persons or their family members provide information about them. Once these specific reactions in a individual are known, music can be used to facilitate a transition from one emotion to another or to stimulate an emotional response in someone with an otherwise flat affect.

Music as Communication. As with all art forms, music is unique communication. What it conveys cannot be better done in any other way or by any other medium. This communication may be either through words of a song in a melodic context or it may be completely nonverbal, relying totally upon one or more musical elements. Using music with persons who are nonverbal or who have communication deficits facilitates their social interaction with others. Music may be the only medium through which some persons can interact with others and feel a part of a group. For example, a person who has severe dementia and who has not spoken in several years can shake a maraca or hit a drum in rhythm to music. Because this response is in rhythm, it can occur within the context of a rhythm ensemble; i.e., the person participates successfully with others. The music, therefore, provides the structure necessary for interacting with others. Through its structure music taps residual communication skills and abilities, even in those who have severe dementia, which can be used for successful group participation. This success with others leads to feelings of belonging and of being needed which are so essential to well being and life quality.

Emotional Expression. Since music can be used as a form of nonverbal communication, it is particularly helpful as a form of expression for those who have limited or no verbal communication skills. Music may be used to express a wide variety of emotions which range from anger and frustration to affection and tenderness. These expressions can take the form of vocalizations which may or may not require words. They can also be formalized through instrument playing, physical movements and facial expressions which are acceptable within the music therapy framework.

Associations with Music. One of the aspects of music which makes it unique to each individual person is the associations that person makes with a particular piece of music. The music may provoke memories of times, places and persons. The association may be direct or indirect. That is, the music may have been heard only in one context or situation and whenever it is heard it is a reminder of that particular moment in time. Or, a piece of music may have a certain style that is more generally associated with a time period in one's life. These associations may be very happy or very sad and even remorseful. They are so individual that they are impossible to predict, and one song that evokes smiles and apparent happiness for one person may trigger tears and apparent grief for another. As with music preferences, some information about a person's reactions to particular music may be obtained. Again, it is important to observe behavioral indications of reactions, whether they are verbal or nonverbal.

Because of strong associations with it, music is often used as a stimulus for reminiscence and life review in elderly persons. Music which was part of the participants' experiences throughout their lifetimes can be selected for this purpose. Observation shows that persons who have lost the communication skills to discuss their lifetimes, can sometimes still sing the songs which were part of their earlier lives and part of their young adult years. But, when those singing skills are also gone, the person may continue to enjoy hearing the songs, particularly if they are sung by someone sitting close who makes eye contact and communicates an attitude of acceptance.

Music and Relaxation. Because music has the capacity to affect physiological responses and because of pleasant associations persons may have with it, music can be a source of relaxation. The proper music played as background in certain settings can promote relief from tension and anxiety. It can quiet agitation and promote comfort. In addition, singing or playing music can function to divert attention from stressors and promote relaxation through relief from stress.

Music in Entertainment and Leisure. Some persons, including some elderly persons, have great amounts of unstructured time in their day. Music provides meaningful, purposeful activities which are enjoyable and constructive uses of time. If the person is emotionally or physically disabled, or if the person has a dementia, music can be used by the caregiver to provide diversion from routinized activities and as a pleasant way to interact with their care receivers.

Music used in entertainment and leisure can include singing, playing or listening activities which are structured around familiar music. Sitting in a chair listening to 20 or 30 minutes of music once or twice a day can provide some opportunity for purposeful activity which requires little effort or skill. While listening, an individual may sing along with certain songs, may tap a foot or a knee in rhythm with the music or may play an instrumental accompaniment.

Music videos provide another enjoyable and constructive use of leisure time. These may include video tapes of musical shows, movies which feature song and dance numbers, musical television programs such a Lawrence Welk or Hee Haw and any other musical programming the person has enjoyed.

While music can provide constructive, meaningful uses of leisure time, it can also lose its effectiveness if used continually. With the constant use of music, individuals become attenuated and lose interest. Consequently, the music becomes ineffective. If the use of music is interrupted periodically throughout the day with silence or other activities, the music maintains its effectiveness in focusing attention, providing sensory stimulation, offering diversion from routine and providing meaningful uses of leisure time.

Why Music Works

Music is Flexible. Music activities can be designed to provide success for persons of various physiological, psychological and social response levels even when they are severely dysfuncitonal. Successful experiences are difficult for severely dysfunctional persons, yet, they are essential to feelings of well being. If a severely dysfunctional person cannot experience success in a music activity, then it is the music activity which is not properly designed and not the functioning level of the individual which prohibits the success.

Success in music activities can be defined in a variety of ways depending upon the skills and abilities of the individual for whom they were designed. Successful musical experiences can range form sitting quietly in a chair to actively playing an instrument or singing. For some, success is defined as staying in the room while a music activity is conducted; for others, success is defined as singing an original verse of a song.

Music is Structured and Occurs Through Time. Music is structured and, therefore, predictable. It has predictability whether or not it is familiar because one beat always follows the next. When the music is familiar, then not only the beats follow in a predictable manner but other musical elements also occur predictably. These elements include, among others, melody lines, rhythm patterns, harmonies, textures, timbres and dynamics.

Music can only occur through time and it is perceived only through time. The predictability inherent in music provides for structured time. It is this structure that provides opportunities for anxiety control in those who can no longer maintain their own structure. The predictability also provides opportunities for cooperation with others in reality oriented activities.

Cooperation with others leads to conjoint participation in activities with them. This results in relief from isolation. Opportunities to participate with others are rare in persons who are isolated due to their inabilities to initiate or respond to most social interactions. Through structured opportunities for cooperation individuals can accept responsibility for their behaviors in the activity and for their behaviors which relate to others. They become aware of what they contribute and they become aware of others. This awareness of others is quite rare in severely dysfunctional persons including those with dementia, but it is necessary for their feelings of belonging which are essential to their well being.

Music Therapy with the Elderly: An Overview

It has long been known that opportunities for social interaction and integration into communities contributes to the quality of life for most persons. Some persons maintain their opportunities for social interaction as they age, but some cannot due to caregiving responsibilities of a spouse or other family member, chronic physical disabilities, poor health, inadequate resources and other reasons. Those persons who have fewer and fewer opportunities for social interactions tend to become progressively more isolated. With isolation and feelings of helplessness there is a concomitant feeling of depression (Russell, et al., 1980). This depression increases inversely with increased losses of independence, home, friends, community, mobility, health and with other losses and disappointments. Hanser (1989 and 1990a) has demonstrated that music therapy techniques are very effective for older persons with depression. She provided a music listening program which served as a stimulus for relaxation and pleasant visual images. She reported that these elderly persons had a relief from anxiety symptoms and depression while their self-esteem improved as they participated once weekly for one hour over an eight-week music therapy program (Hanser, 1990b).

Music has always been a viable medium for bringing people together, young and old, for social interaction in a wide variety of contexts. The approach, however, with most persons is to use music in traditional ways, such as instrumental performances as soloists and as members of instrumental and vocal ensembles, church choirs and other choral singing opportunities. While these traditional methods are viable for those who have had opportunities to study music as young persons and who have used these skills throughout their life times, there are often not entry opportunities for those who would like to develop skills as musical performers in later, or even late, life. There is evidence that these older persons are not satisfied with their current musical skill levels and would like better ones. They are also concerned about good musical products (Gibbons, 1982). They are not pleased with mediocre performances or instruction and are quick to respond with verbal displeasure when they perceive either. They are sensitive, as they should be, about their dignity and do not respond well to situations in which they are spoken "down to" or in which they feel they are treated without respect appropriate for an adult. Therefore, music programs which include "toy" instruments, kitchen pots and wooden spoons and songs of childhood, along with "silly" costumes and any other demeaning activities are totally unacceptable.

When given a supportive environment in which they are allowed and encouraged to develop, there is also research and practice evidence that older persons have the abilities to learn musical skills through their late life years (Gibbons, 1982). When they participate in these programs focused on musical skill development they demand challenging instruction and work eagerly to improve their performances. As a result they can learn new skills, or can relearn those acquired much earlier in life, quite successfully (Gibbons, 1984). Even when these persons are so frail that they must reside in a care home, research shows they still have the abilities to learn new musical skills, provided they have sufficient congnitive functioning (Gibbons, 1983a, 1983b).

So, what about music performance contributes therapeutically to elderly persons' quality of life? When asked this question those who use music make comments which include: "When I play/sing music with others, I have an opportunity to work together with them to do something I really enjoy." Or, "Music gives me a great excuse to call someone and get together". And, "Music just makes me feel so good, especially when our group sounds great!" Or, "I use music to pass the time, I have a lot of it on my hands and I don't get around like I used to. Music gives me a great way to fill my day." One 82-year-old man said, "I like to perform the music for others and I think it is important to do it in nursing homes, too, for those people who are less fortunate than us." One widow woman who lived alone in a stone farm house in Kansas said, " When I feel bad I play my guitar and wail the blues and when I feel good, I do more joyful songs." She said that it didn't matter how her music sounded, because the singing and playing was important to her-- besides, she said, the dog kind of seemed to like it.

These comments all came from people who learned musical skills when they were over 70, and some were over 80, years old. They continued regular music rehearsals and performances after the program in which they learned the skills was discontinued. They were able to develop enough independence and confidence through the music therapy program that they successfully organized themselves into a well determined group of musical performers.

Therapeutic Music Programs for the Elderly

The goals for life quality change according to individual needs and desires, and are conjointly dependent on the resources available. An extensive review of the literature indicates music is effective in a wide range of programming (Gibbons, 1988). The focus of this presentation is the therapeutic use of music with the elderly, a population that has a broad range of needs and concerns which shift as their lives change with age.

Music with the Well Elderly

My experience with elderly persons and the therapeutic uses of music began with an experimental program I developed at the University of Kansas, Lawrence, Kansas in 1977 for well, elderly persons who were interested in developing music skills. In this program elderly persons studied individually or in small groups with a music instructor to either develop new musical skills or to relearn those skills learned much earlier in life, sometimes more than 50 years earlier. These skills were applied in a weekly group music session in which as many as 25 to 30 people participated together in a vocal/instrumental ensemble. As individuals' skills developed in the music sessions, they were incorporated at a comparable skill level in the music ensemble. This music ensemble gave 10 to 15 public performances each year of its existence in the Lawrence, Kansas community, and was invited to perform at the Kansas Govenor's Conference on Aging in 1979.

This music therapy program was free to participants and was run entirely by volunteer instructors. Without funding and with demands on time, the program was discontinued. It served, however, as a useful resource in the community for eight years. Its goals were focused on life enrichment and intellectual stimulation, the development of social/musical networks, self-esteem and feelings of worth through successful experiences and opportunities for developing life satisfaction.

This preliminary work using music with well elderly has demonstrated that music can contribute to the life quality of this population. Further study of this area is needed to provide more comprehensive knowledge of the uses of music in personal development and fulfillment.

The Chronically Ill Elderly at Home

Most elderly persons do not require full time residential care and live at home. Many of these older persons are physically fit and active in a wide range of social contacts, but others become isolated at home because of various disabling diseases and physical changes. Many of these conditions become chronic and lead, eventually, to terminal illnesses.

Music therapy has long been a viable therapeutic approach with frail elderly in residential care facilities (Gibbons, 1988), and these applications are also possible in individuals' private homes. Problems come with access and availability, however. Programs to train family members or volunteers to use music therapy services with their elderly loved ones would be economically feasible, but these programs are in the conceptual stages. If family members/volunteers could be trained to implement programs under the supervision of a music therapist, music programming could be effective and efficient in the home setting. In addition, the music could provide opportunities for families to interact around activities for which the chronically ill, elderly member is capable socially, physically and psychologically.

As an alternative to residential care home placement, many families are considering maintaining their elderly loved one at home and placing them in day care during the work day. Day care can also provide respite for caregivers who need some time to perform household responsibilities or to just rest from the burdens of caregiving. Music therapy programs can be implemented in day care similar to the ones provided in residential care home facilities. They may or may not involve the individual's family members.

Yet, still other chronically ill elderly persons are afflicted with a terminal disease and choose to spend their last days in their own homes. Music therapy is new in the area of terminal illness management and treatment. Some preliminary clinical work has shown that music can provide diversion from chronic pain and provide for relaxation for those who are in the late stages of a terminal illness. Besides pain management and diversion, music therapy probably has an important role in managing and/or treating chronic illness as a medium which provides opportunities for families to deal with the emotional impact of the disease. It enables families to interact and reminisce together while including the ill family member. Music can provide a means for communicating those feelings and emotions which are painful, but also those which are associated with happier times throughout the family history. Through song writing and other approaches, music therapy can serve to record and communicate family information and emotions and can draw the family members together to share it.

Again, the full impact of music with the ill elderly at home will be known through additional study and research. Preliminary work has shown potential, but this area is generally unexplored.

Music Therapy with Frail, Elderly Care Home Residents

In the eight years the music therapy /music development program was implemented for well elderly, I was also developing other music therapy programming in residential care facilities, otherwise known as nursing homes. These programs focused on the maintenance of musical skills in those who were no longer living in their own homes, and the use of those skills to provide opportunities for social interaction, cooperation with others, awareness of self and others, and feelings of belonging. Though this population had clear indications of musical abilities (Gibbons, 1983a; 1983b), they had some difficulties executing them (Clair, 1991) probably because of their serious physical, and sometimes emotional, disabilities. Consequently, these elderly persons were not usually candidates to learn new music performance skills. They did, however, learn new ways to incorporate the skills they had into new music activities and contexts and often did not require the amount of supervision or assistance that care home staff indicated they needed (Clair, 1990). For them the program design entailed participation in small groups of 6 to 10 persons once or twice a week and involvement in a large, all resident, community music therapy session at least once weekly. Small group activities included using music to 1) reminisce and subsequently discuss life satisfaction and life quality, 2) manage stress and sleeplessness, 3) interact musically together in an ensemble, 4) stimulate the senses through auditory, tactile and visual media and to 5) motivate involvement and integration with others. Goals were often centered around the development of maintaining as much control and independence in life as possible through decision making, feeling needed by others, sensory and cognitive awareness, social integration into the care home community, self-esteem and feelings of respect and dignity, and satisfaction with current life.

<u>Music Therapy with Elderly Persons with Dementia and their Families</u>

Estimates indicate that half the elderly persons in the United States who require residential care suffer from an irreversible dementia called Alzheimer's disease (Reisberg, 1983; Schneider & Emr, 1985). This disease is on the upswing and epidemiological studies in the United States, Great Britain and Scandinavia estimate that five to seven percent of those persons over age 65 and 20 percent of those over age 80 have it (Mortimer & Hutton, In Press). With this diagnosis individuals can live 7 to 10 years, and sometimes more, with a disease that is terminal. As these persons progress through the disease, they become more and more dysfunctional. As a consequence, their quality of life and the quality of life of those who care for them deteriorates continually.

Family caregivers become isolated due to the strain of constant care when the person with dementia is maintained at home. And, even when the individual must be moved to a residential care facility, the family caregiver has the burden of emotional and financial support. These persons continue to experience the losses of social contacts in the community suffered through months and years of isolation. They also are at risk for physical illnesses (Light & Leibowitz, 1989) and depression (Boss, et al., 1990) due to the stresses of caregiving. The consequences of this disease, and other dementias, are devastating.

In the last four years I have been developing, along with my colleague, Barry Bernstein, RMT-BC, music therapy practice protocols and research with elderly persons diagnosed with dementias, primarily of the Alzheimer's type. In the last year we have expanded our work to include family members and have consulted with colleague Susan Tebb, MSW to develop a music therapy program for persons with dementia and their spouse caregivers.

The focus of the earliest work was the development of programs for those persons who were so severely regressed that they could no longer function in their homes, and they had to reside in a care facility where their needs for constant care and safety could best be met. This work included the development of music therapy programs which have involved these persons in participation with one another and with family members who visited the facility. Based on three years of clinical work, a music therapy practice protocol was developed. It will be published along with a music therapy practice protocol developed by Hanser for persons who are mildly afflicted with the disease in the early stages (Clair & Hanser, In Press).

Most of the severely regressed patients with whom we work are so debilitated that many of them do not speak, and if they do their speech is unintelligible. They are also emotionally labile and their emotional responses are often not appropriate or predictable. Many of them do not have bowel or bladder control, some of them need help feeding themselves, they all need help with bathing and dressing and they are not going to get better. They will get more and more isolated and withdrawn, they will forget how to walk and eventually how to eat and how to swallow. They will probably get a respiratory disease and die. Until then, they will require complete and continuous care to merely exist.

The quality of these patients' lives will continue to decline. They do not remember the names of their children or their spouses. They no longer respond to the family dog when it is brought to visit at the hospital, even though it was once an endeared pet. But, they still seem to recognize a familiar face even though their ability to learn and remember names has long gone.

In the music therapy sessions, these persons play/make music together using percussion instruments and upon initial admission to the hospital some of them still sing. Eventually they become debilitated until they can no longer sing but they can and do still play a rhythm instrument (Clair & Bernstein, 1990) They also participate in moving their bodies in rhythm to the music, to dance at first, and later after much deterioration, in rhythmic arm swinging in response to music. Eventually they participate by just staying in the room and making eye contact. Even this very basic level of involvement is significant since these patients get to the point they can no longer participate in any other activities. One patient, who had gotten to the point that he could no longer communicate in any way, still came to the music therapy sessions. He always made eye contact when the music therapist sat close by and sang to him. Eventually he became very ill and was hospitalized with a critical respiratory infection. He appeared to be sleeping most of the time but when his wife sang to him, he opened his eyes and looked at her. On the last day he lived she was with him in his hospital room, she sang his favorite hymn, he opened his eyes and looked at her for the last time. It was, she said, something she will never forget--a moment that happened because she sang to him.

The persons with severe dementia with whom we have worked participate best in rhythm activities that involve vibrotactile stimulation, or the vibration that results from percussive sounds (Clair & Bernstein, 1990a; 1990b; Unpublished Paper b). The most viable activity to date has been the use of flat drums which can be held in the hand or placed in the lap and played either with hands or mallets. The drum playing seems rather reflexive in patients who are severely regressed in the disease. They quickly begin to strike the drum when it is handed to them, even if they have had no prior experience with it. This drum playing, when done with simple repeated beats, does not seem to require a high level of cognitive organization. But, even very regressed persons can cognitively organize well enough to learn new rhythm patterns, to imitate a pattern played by some one else or to play in some way other than his/her initial response (Clair & Bernstein, 1989). These persons illustrate well the principle that all persons can participate in music provided it is adjusted to suit their functional behaviors.

The clinical work we have done has indicated that persons with severe deterioration due to dementias can learn to participate in music activities particularly when they are included in small groups of five to seven persons for a period of several weeks. Their responses in the small groups seem to generalize and they can eventually participate in activities in much larger groups; i.e., when the entire hospital unit is included, 26 to 28 persons. Even in the small group activities, however, persons seem to be somewhat agitated initially. This may be due to the threat of a new environment, the change in routine or the presentation of a new activity. Once the individuals experience success with music in the small groups, they settle down and participate for as long as 30 minutes, a duration of attention that is quite unusual in this population (Clair & Bernstein, 1990c). The nurses on the unit where the sessions are held say that the only time the patients all come into the day room and sit down is when the music therapists come to do a session. Nursing staff and spouses who observe the music therapy sessions say that patients seem more alert during and following the music therapy sessions. They also say that the patients tend to settle down with music. There is no research which indicates music has lasting effects on persons with dementia, but preliminary observations indicate it is an area worthy of study. An initial study of the effects of music on agitated behaviors did not provide definitive results (Clair & Bernstein, Unpublished Paper a), and, subsequently, this is an area that requires further research.

In the last year the music therapy work has expanded to include spouses or other family caregivers in the sessions. Couples participate in groups in which singing, drum playing and dancing are programmed. These caregivers have told us that in music therapy their loved ones have reacted much the way they did in the past and that they could see snatches of who these people used to be. They were quite excited that we could tap the residual skills and abilities along with the personality traits they had watched disappear before their eyes. One wife told us after dancing with her husband for the first time in many years, "Oh, he held me in his arms. It has been such a long time since he just held me." The music provided the structure in which he could hold her and resume some of his behaviors from long ago, the behaviors that were such an integral part of the intimacy of their relationship. The parts that should still be there, but most of the time they are not, because her husband has a dementia, probably of the Alzheimer's type.

Most recently, Barry Bernstein, Susan Tebb, MSW and I tested our music therapy practice protocol for caregivers with persons who were diagnosed with dementia, probably of the Alzheimer's type, who still resided in their own homes. These persons were living with spouses who were their primary caregivers and who participated with them in the music therapy programming. Four caregivers and their spouses diagnosed with dementia in the middle stages participated successfully together in singing, rhythm drumming and dancing activities, for 30 minutes each week for six weeks.

The afflicted spouses in these sessions were still living at home, but were very dysfunctional. They needed help and/or supervision for even the most basic activities of daily living; i.e., eating, bathing, dressing and going to the toilet. They could no longer participate as a viable member of the couple, but could still be maintained at home as long as they had constant supervision. They could no longer participate in couple activities. Even so, when familiar songs were introduced in the sessions, all participants attempted to sing for some or all of the songs. They responded particularly well to playing drums, even though they had no prior experience playing them. The persons with dementia took the drums willingly and used them to interact, playing rhythmically within the group. When the dancing portion of the session came, afflicted spouses took their caregiving spouses in their arms, the ladies tucked their heads under the chins of their husbands, and they danced to big band music of their young adult years..., just as they had done in their early years together. Caregivers reported that they were using some of the activities at home with their spouses. One lady said that she and her husband had begun dancing in the kitchen, an activity they had long given up doing in public.

It is clear through our clinical work and research that music influences positively the activity levels of persons with dementia, even when they are severely regressed. Even though they do not participate in other activities, they can still play an instrument rhythmically and they can still dance. If they have had no experience with dancing, prior to the onset of the disease, they can still swing arms and move their feet in rhythm to the music. It is the music that seems to integrate them into activity with others. It reduces their isolation for a time, though it may be only a short time, and consequently it influences the quality of their lives. At the same time, it provides opportunities for family caregivers to participate with their afflicted family members in a purposeful, productive way. Through well-designed and implemented music therapy activities, they can again make contact with their loved ones. They can use the music to relate positively with whatever residual skills are left.

We think it is very possible that spouses and other family caregivers can learn to use music with their afflicted family members provided they have the appropriate training and supervision. We have established practice protocols, for both severely deteriorated and moderately deteriorated individuals, which could provide the framework for the training. With this training services can be extended to a much broader portion of the population afflicted with the disease. It is even possible that such training programs could make these services available to those in rural areas. This training, integrated with research to study its effectiveness, can make approaches to therapeutic uses of music available to families that are devastated by one of the most dreaded diseases in this country, dementia.

Music Therapy for the Caregiver

There is a growing body of literature which describes the terrible devastation suffered by those families, and particularly by those older caregivers of persons with dementia.. This literature indicates stress, depression, poor physical care, emotional distress and other factors which lead to the breakdown of health, life satisfaction and quality of life. The music therapy project we conducted in the past year has led to some preliminary program design for caregivers. The therapeutic uses of music to manage stress, promote relaxation and provide opportunities for self development and fulfillment are areas for study and program development. This work should be a priority along with the use of music in the treatment of persons with dementia.

Conclusion

I give this testimony as a professional music therapist, and I do not speak for the University of Kansas or for the Veterans Affairs Medical Center where I now do music therapy practice and research. This testimony is therefore limited to the work of one individual and some of the professional literature which supports it. There is much more research which points clearly to the positive, effects of therapeutic uses of music on the elderly. Even with its limited scope, the research and clinical practice reported here have demonstrated that music has therapeutic effects on elderly persons, and sometimes these effects are quite remarkable. Additional clinical work and research are needed to more fully describe the musical characteristics and the effects of music on elderly persons and their families so that appropriate programming may be designed and implemented in the most effective and efficient ways.

References

Boss, P., Caron, W., Horbal, J., & Mortimer, J. (1990). Predictors of depression in caregivers of dementia patients: Boundary ambiguity and mastery. Family Process, 29, 245-254.

Clair, A. A. (In Press). Music therapy for a severely regressed person with a probable diagnosis of Alzheimer's disease: A case study. In K. Bruscia (Ed.). Case studies in music therapy.

Clair, A.A. (1991). Rhythmic responses in elderly and their implications for music therapy practice. Journal of the International Association of Music for the Handicapped, 6, 3-11.

Clair, A.A. (1990). The need for supervision to manage behavior in the elderly care home resident and the implications for music therapy practice. Music Therapy Perspectives, 8, 72-75.

Clair, A.A., & Bernstein, B. (1989). "A caregivers' guide to using music with persons who have severe dementia: An introduction". Unpublished manuscript, Colmery-O'Neil Veterans Affairs Medical Center, Topeka, Kansas.

Clair, A. A. & Bernstein, B. (1990a). A comparison of singing, vibrotactile and nonvibrotactile instrumental playing responses in severely regressed persons with dementia of the Alzheimer's type. [Abstract]. The Gerontologist, 30, 22A

Clair, A. A. & Bernstein, B. (1990b). A comparison of singing, vibrotactile and nonvibrotactile instrumental playing responses in severely regressed persons with dementia of the Alzheimer's type. Journal of Music Therapy, 27, 119-125.

Clair, A. A. & Bernstein, B. (1990c). A preliminary study of music therapy programming for severely regressed persons with Alzheimer's type dementia. Journal of Applied Gerontology, 9, 299-311.

Clair, A. A. & Bernstein, B. (Unpublished paper a) "The effect of no music, stimulative music and sedative music on agitated behaviors in persons with severe dementia." Submitted for publication to The Journal of Music Therapy.

Clair, A. A., & Bernstein, B. (Unpublished paper b) "The performance for vibrotactile versus auditory stimuli in severely regressed persons with dementia of the Alzheimer's type compared with dementia due to ethanol abuse." Submitted for publication to The American Journal of Alzheimer's Care and Related Disorders and Research.

Clair, A. A. was formerly Gibbons, A. C.

Gibbons, A.C. (1984). A program for non-institutionalized, mature adults: A description. Activities Adaptation and Aging, 6, 71-80.

Gibbons, A. C. (1988). A review of literature for music development/education and music therapy with the elderly. Music Therapy Perspectives, 5, 33-40.

Gibbons, A.C. (1983a). Item analysis of the *PRIMARY MEASURES OF MUSIC AUDIATION* in elderly care home residents. Journal of Music Therapy, 20, 201-210.

Gibbons, A.C. (1982). *MUSICAL APTITUDE PROFILE* scores in a non-institutionalized elderly population. Journal of Research in Music Education, 30, 23-29.

Gibbons, A.C. (1984). Music development in the elderly: What are the chances? Design, 86, 24-25.

Gibbons, A.C. (1982). Music skill level self-evaluation in non-institutionalized elderly. Activities Adaptation and Aging, 3, 61-67.

Gibbons, A.C. (1977). Popular musical preferences of elderly persons. Journal of Music Therapy, 14, 180-189.

Gibbons, A.C. (1983b). *PRIMARY MEASURES OF MUSIC AUDIATION* scores in an institutionalized elderly population. Journal of Music Therapy, 20, 21-29.

Gibbons, A.C. (1988). Some perceptions of music therapy. Journal of the International Association of Music for the Handicapped, 1, 3-10.

Gibbons, A.C. (1985). Stop babying the elderly. Music Educators Journal, 71, 48-51. (This article is an adaptation of one appearing in Design, 1984, 86, 24-25.)

Gibbons, A.C. & Heller, G.N. (1985). Music Therapy in Handel's England. College Music Symposium, 25, 59-72.

Hanser, S. B. (1990a). A music therapy strategy for depressed older adults in the community. Journal of Applied Gerontology, 9, 283-298.

Hanser, S. B. (1990b). Two investigations of the impact of music on older adults in the community. (Unpublished Paper) Presented at the XIX Conference of the International Society for Music Education, Helsinki, Finland, August, 1990.

Hanser, S. B. (1989). Music therapy with depressed older adults. Journal of the International Association for music for the Handicapped, 4, 15-26.

Hanser, S. B. & Clair, A. A.(In Press). Music therapy: Returning the losses of dementia of the Alzheimer's type for patient and caregiver. In T. Wigram, R. West and B. Saperston (Eds.). Music and the healing process: A handbook of music therapy.

Light, E., & Leibowitz, B. D. (1989). Alzheimer's disease treatment and family stress: Directions for research. Rockville, Maryland: U. S. Department of Health and Human Services.

Mortimer, J. A., & Hutton J. T. (In Press). Epidemiology and etiology of Alzheimer's disease. In J. T. Hutton & A. D. Keany (Eds.). Senile dementia of the Alzheimer type. New York: Alan R. Liss, Inc.

Reisberg, B. (1983). A guide to Alzheimer's disease. New York: Free Press.

Russell, D., Peplau, L. A., & Cutrona, C. E. (1980). The revised UCLA loneliness scale: Concurrent and discriminant validity evidence. Journal of Personality and Social Psychology, 39, 475.

Schneider, E. L., & Emr, M. (1985, May/June). Alzheimer's disease: Research highlights. Geriatric Nursing, 136-138.

Standley, J. M. (1986). Music research in medical/dental treatment: Meta-analysis and clinical applications. Journal of Music Therapy, 23, 56-122.

National Association for Music Therapy, Inc.

8455 COLESVILLE ROAD   SILVER SPRING, MD 20910   (301) 589-3300   FAX (301) 589-5175

Music Therapy Services for Older Adults

RESEARCH AGENDA

The efficacy of music therapy has been demonstrated through extensive clinical practice. Model demonstration projects, basic research and clinical outcome research can extend and further validate music therapy applications.

Future research will encompass populations of older Americans such as, but not limited to, those with Alzheimer's disease and other dementias, those with neurological disorders associated with aging such as stroke and Parkinson's disease, those with psychiatric disorders, and older persons institutionalized with other debilitating conditions. In addition, research is needed to study the effects of music with professional and family caregivers, and in preventive care for well, older Americans. Music's potential as a diagnostic tool, especially of cognitive functioning levels, should also be explored.

Settings for clinical research include residential care, adult day care, inpatient and outpatient rehabilitation, home health care, and senior citizens and retirement communities in urban and rural settings. Areas of research may include, but not be limited to:

1. The effect of music on neurological functioning, communication skills and physical rehabilitation in older adults.

2. The effect of music therapy interventions on hospitalized older adults and those experiencing pain.

3. The effect of music therapy interventions on cognitive, emotional, and social functioning in those with Alzheimer's disease and related dementias.

4. The effect of music therapy interventions on the emotional and social well-being of caregivers and families of those with cognitive and physical impairments.

5. The effect of music therapy interventions on depressed/anxious older adults.

6. The effect of music therapy interventions on life satisfaction and life quality in older adults.

7. The effect of music therapy interventions on disease prevention and general health of older adults.

The studies listed below are examples of research which would be facilitated with modest federal support. Many of the studies have already been pilot-tested with positive results, and they await replication and expansion. The list contained herein is by no means exhaustive.

RESEARCH AREA ONE

The Effect of Music Therapy Interventions on Neurological Functioning, Communication Skills, and Physical Rehabilitation in Older Adults

Proposed Study #1: "The influence of music on brain wave activity in the severely regressed patient with dementia."

A large body of literature has examined the effect of music on brain processes (Gates and Bradshaw, 1977). In dementia patients, observation and clinical case studies have shown that persons in the late stage of dementia, including dementia of the Alzheimer's type, are unresponsive to all stimuli except music. (Norberg, et. al., 1986). This study would examine, through the use of EEG measurement, the possibility of brain activity of severely regressed dementia patients in response to musical stimuli, which would indicate whether or not the patient has potential for response to music therapy interventions.

Proposed Study #2: "Musical responses as indicators of function and dysfunction in late stage dementia."

Dementia of the Alzheimer's type is characterized by predictable decline in a variety of functional areas. Research has indicated that this decline may manifest itself via musical behavior (Clair and Bernstein, 1990). Clinical observations have shown that declines in skills such as singing and dancing may progress at a slower rate than declines in other areas of cognitive functioning. A longitudinal approach in this study would construct a profile of musical responses characteristic of each stage of the disease. Such a profile would assist the music therapy practitioner in planning intervention strategies appropriate for patients at each of these stages.

Proposed Study #3: "The effects of melodic intonation therapy on communication skills of older stroke victims and those with Parkinson's disease."

Melodic intonation therapy is effective in reestablishing communication skills in younger populations. (Lucia, 1987). Pilot tests using this technique with older stroke victims have been positive. Controlled studies using adaptations of Melodic Intonation Therapy and other music therapy interventions are needed to test effects on articulation, breath control and communication in both institutionalized and community dwelling older adults with conditions affecting communication.

Proposed Study #4: "Recall of song lyrics as indicative of memory functioning levels."

While most individuals will complain of problems remembering information, in the majority of cases these difficulties would not be classified as serious. The recall of song lyrics might provide a means for assessing the severity of memory impairment, as well as a context for learning adaptive memory strategies.

Proposed Study #5: "The effects of music on the organization of thought processes in individuals with dementia."

It has been observed that after participating in music experiences, individuals with dementia often manifest increased verbal clarity. Studies could be developed which would investigate physiological/neurological processes operating to produce this phenomenon.

Proposed Study #6: "The effect of music on gait training for those in stroke rehabilitation programs."

A. Music has been shown to be effective in prolonging physical activity, facilitating efficient muscle firing, reducing the perception of pain, and equalizing stride width and length. (Staum, 1983). Music may be effective in improving the gait of stroke victims with partial paralysis by facilitating endurance in physical activity and equi-distance of footfalls, and by improving the older adult's mental attitude about rehabilitation. The effect of rhythmic gait training on prevention of falls is also of interest.

B. Rhythm, in the form of metronome beats and musical patterns, has been used as a pacing signal to influence the timing, velocity, cadence speed and rhythmicity of movement. (Thaut, 1991). The effectiveness of this technique should be compared to standard physical therapy protocols in the rehabilitation of both gait and upper extremity disorders. The timing and magnitude of EMG activity in response to rhythmic signals is another area for investigation.

Proposed Study #7: "The effect of music and rhythm in the rehabilitation of older adults."

A. Event-related brain potentials are beginning to be studied in the perception of auditory rhythm. New research would measure ERP's while older and younger adults 1) listen to auditory beat, 2) perform a motor task without beat, 3) perform a task with rhythmic cue, 4) perform with an intermittent anticipatory beat, 5) follow an irregular rhythm, 6) follow rhythms which gradually speed up or slow down.

B. People afflicted with Parkinson's disease have great difficulty with motor initiation and termination. Efficient techniques of cueing motor behavior are in great need. The effects of auditory rhythmic stimulus "sensory trigger" cues to facilitate the initiation of movement in those with Parkinson's disease must be studied.

C. Though basic research has been done on the effects of music on muscle relaxation (Scartelli, 1984), there is need to study the interaction between the auditory system and the motor system. The influence of sound stimuli on EMG amplitude modulation and latent period in motor reactions should be examined in both normal and impaired individuals. Study of auditory rhythmic input on neural activity in descending motor pathways would elucidate some of the audio-spinal motor interactions underlying clinical applications.

D. Case studies have shown music skill instruction on the piano to be an effective means to regain the use of muscles mildly paralyzed by stroke in community dwelling elderly individuals. Information concerning the role of previous musical experience and motivation, instruction on various instruments, and the extent of paralysis on rehabilitation needs to be explored. Similar effects on individuals suffering from arthritis may be studied.

Proposed Study #8: "The use of musical stimuli and music therapy interventions in the reality orientation of older adults."

Pilot data have shown that the principles of reality orientation (orientation to person, place and time) can be integrated into individual and group music activities. (Riegler, 1980). Musical stimuli (i.e. songs about the season, the place, a particular holiday) and structured musical activities that require attention to person, place, and time offer numerous opportunities for reality orientation in a natural social environment. Additional investigation can help determine those interventions most effective for persons at different levels of cognitive functioning both in group and individual therapy.

<u>Proposed Study #9</u>: "Physiological measurement of responsiveness to music"

While clinical evidence clearly establishes a responsiveness to music by severely cognitively impaired individuals, only one study sponsored by NIA is attempting to document these changes. Event-related potentials are being investigated in Alzheimer's patients, but this research will only begin to determine whether the processing of musical stimuli can be observed in this way. Extensive research using the latest technology, including PET scans, potentials in the brain and other physiological measurement devices, is needed to help understand how the brain processes music and its effectiveness as a therapeutic tool.

<u>Proposed Study #10</u>: "The effects of music therapy interventions on respiratory efficiency in older adults."

Acute and chronic respiratory conditions are frequent problems for older adults. It is well known that vital capacity and the structures around the lungs which support respiratory processes decrease with age. It has also been demonstrated that training in singing can enhance respiratory functioning. (Gould and Okamura, 1973). Studies could be developed which would a) assess the effects of training in singing on the respiratory efficiency of older adults and b) assess the efficacy of singing experiences on the amelioration of breathing difficulties associated with respiratory pathology.

<u>Proposed Study #11</u>: "The use of singing in the treatment of SDB associated with Alzheimer's disease"

A relationship has been established between the condition of sleep-disordered breathing (SDB) and levels of dementia in older adults. (Berry, 1988). Studies could be developed which would determine whether or not therapeutic singing experiences could ameliorate respiratory disturbances, and thus contribute to improved sleep behavior.

RESEARCH AREA TWO

The Effect of Music Therapy Interventions on Hospitalized Older Adults and Those Experiencing Pain

<u>Proposed Study #1</u>: "The influence of music on pain perception in older patients with rheumatoid arthritis."

Pilot study results indicate that music vibrations may be a significant factor in the relief of rheumatoid arthritis pain. It is theorized that specific skin sensors, which block pain reception at the spinal level when stimulated, can be activated by specific sound frequencies and amplitudes. Controlled studies need to be undertaken to confirm this effect.

<u>Proposed Study #2</u>: "The influence of music on the amount of post-operative pain medication."

Surgical procedures are followed with pain management medications. This study would examine the influence of music as an alternative to, or as an accompaniment to, medication to reduce the amount of medication needed to promote comfort.

<u>Proposed Study #3</u>: "The influence of music on the amount of medication required to maintain comfort in outpatient surgery."

Some preliminary work has shown that music therapy protocols are effective in managing pain in outpatient surgeries. (Wolfe, 1978). Patients with less medication have lower probabilities of complications resulting from it, consequently they have less need for hospital care following surgery.

<u>Proposed Study #4</u>: "The effect of music therapy interventions on length of hospital stay".

Music therapy services are available in some rehabilitation and recreation departments of general hospitals. In music therapy sessions, patients learn techniques to cope with illness and pain which they can use at home. The impact of these services on length of hospital stay and effective coping at home has yet to be examined.

<u>Proposed Study #5</u>: "The effect of music therapy interventions on immune response"

Music therapy strategies were shown to alter immune responses in young hospitalized patients in one study using salivary IGA. (Rider, 1985). This highly promising area of research requires more extensive studies of older adults and patients with a variety of medical conditions, including cancer and other life-threatening illnesses.

<u>Proposed Study #6</u>: "The effect of music therapy on stress reduction."

Stress contributes to a large percentage of medical illnesses in the country. For example, the risk of cardiovascular disease due to hypertension is great. There is a considerable body of research justifying music therapy interventions for diminishing stress. (Curtis, 1982; Hanser, 1985). However, more research with older adults will determine the efficacy of music-facilitated stress reduction for the problems facing older adults.

Proposed Study #7: "Music vibroacoustic therapy to improve circulation, reduce stress, and diminish effects of arthritis in older adults."

The crippling effect of arthritis can be devastating to otherwise healthy and active older citizens. This innovative technique seems to have clinical value but has yet to be tested in controlled research.

Proposed Study #8: "Guided imagery through music to facilitate a family's coping with terminal illness of a loved one."

Music therapists working in Hospice Centers use techniques of music therapy, guided imagery and life review to assist families in coping with the impending death of a loved one. Documentation of the effects of these programs in facilitating the grief process of the family and the patient's ability to cope with terminal illness must be tested.

Proposed Study #9: "Singing to maintain vital capacity and prevent respiratory illness in individuals with limited mobility."

Singing provides motivation for breathing exercises which assist hospitalized or immobilized (wheelchair bound) older adults prevent respiratory difficulties. The effects of regular singing on adherence to a regimen of respiratory therapy and its eventual impact on lung capacity has not been investigated systematically.

RESEARCH AREA THREE

The Effect of Music on Cognitive, Emotional, and Social Functioning in Those with Alzheimer's Disease and Related Dementias

Proposed Study #1: "Musical task performance as an indication of dementia: A comparison of individual responses."

None of the cognitive assessment tools that are presently in use contain musical components. However, because musical tasks provide a valuable source of non-verbal information, its ability to test cognitive functioning is unique. This study could provide important information concerning the suitability of musical tasks as early predictors of dementia and measurements of mental functioning.

Proposed Study #2: "The influence of music on agitated behaviors in persons diagnosed with late stage dementia"

This study is significant in that agitated behaviors are deleterious to those diagnosed with dementias and those around them. Drugs can be used to calm these person, but often are not adequate in dosages which allow the person to be alert. Case study information and pilot study research (Wylie, 1990; Millard and Smith, 1989) has indicated that music can be effective in reducing agitation. Study needs to be done to document the effectiveness of music in reducing agitation without medication and in conjunction with minimal medication.

Proposed Study #3: "The influence of rhythm and melody to promote responses in persons diagnosed with late stage dementia."

Much of the literature reveals that persons with early stage dementia can sing when they can do nothing else. Clinical observation demonstrates that persons do not sing as their disease progresses, but that they tend to respond consistently to rhythmic activities particularly those which require tactile responses. This study would confirm these observations and help create prescribed music therapy interventions for late stage dementia patients.

Proposed Study #4: "The effect of music therapy interventions on attention, memory, retention of information, and learning in cognitively impaired older adults, particularly those with Alzheimer's disease."

Prior research has shown that music functions to enhance learning rates and memory of children, even those with developmental disabilities. (Gfeller, 1983). Pilot studies with older adults have shown that these music and learning principles may be effective in assisting older adults with retention of skills and information and in the acquisition of new abilities. Habituated, synchronized music/skill routines may be effective in prolonging the period of time during which those with dementia are able to maintain self-care skills and relationships to others. Further, if music can help focus attention, it is possible to achieve greater instructional control.

RESEARCH AREA FOUR

The Effect of Music Therapy Interventions on the Emotional and Social Well-Being of Caregivers and Families of Those with Cognitive and Physical Impairment

Proposed Study #1: "The effect of music therapy interventions on social interactions between caregivers and their loved ones diagnosed with dementia of the Alzheimer's type."

This study is important due to the inability of caregivers to relate to their loved ones who they have observed disintegrate before their eyes. They have lost the usual avenues of communication and are desperate for ways to socially interact with their family member who is afflicted with dementia. Pilot tests have shown that music can provide a means for verbal and nonverbal communication which is integral to the maintenance of the relationship. How this phenomenon occurs would be of interest to researchers. Also of importance would be the development of research-based protocols which music therapists could use to facilitate such communication.

Proposed Study #2: "The effect of music therapy interventions on the well-being of caregivers for those with dementia."

This study would provide essential information on the care and well-being of the caregiver. These persons sacrifice themselves and often their health to provide care for persons who are continually in need of attention. Music therapy strategies provide stress management procedures which help relieve the stress and burden of caregivers. Research will fine-tune these procedures and establish who can benefit most from these music therapy interventions.

Proposed Study #3: "The use of group music activities to promote social behaviors and reduce isolation."

Isolation has been described by some gerontologists as on of the most debilitating factors facing the elderly. Not only can isolation contribute to feelings of depression, but failure to engage in meaningful activities can contribute to helplessness and deterioration. Music activities have been used to assist older adults in developing communication skills to facilitate social interaction. (Redinbaugh, 1988). This study would examine those adaptations and organizational factors most important in sustaining active and meaningful involvement and identify those factors in group music activities.

RESEARCH AREA FIVE

The Effect of Music Therapy on Depressed/Anxious Older Adults

Proposed Study #1: "The influence of music therapy programming on depression in older adults"

This study can be conducted with older adults living in their own homes and with those institutionalized in residential care. Both populations of older persons have high incidence of depression. Preliminary research sponsored by NIA has shown that music therapy procedures may lower depression and anxiety while improving self-esteem. Further research will expand applications of this model and identify under which circumstances the techniques work best.

Proposed Study #2: "Music therapy interventions as a means to reach homebound older adults."

A tremendously underserved group consists of older adults who are homebound due to physical illness, depression, anxiety or lack of access to transportation to more formal services. These older adults may be trained to use music therapy techniques at home to help relieve symptoms of anxiety and depression and help them cope with their problems. Preliminary research, sponsored by NIA, has demonstrated the efficacy of these techniques with a small sample. More study will identify the elements of these methods with the greatest application to a large group of people in an attempt to delay or prevent their placement in nursing homes or long-term care facilities.

RESEARCH AREA SIX

The Effect of Music Therapy Experiences on Life Satisfaction and Life Quality in Older Adults

Proposed Study #1: "The effects of developing new and previously learned music skills on self-esteem and self-efficacy in older adults."

This study would examine the development of musical skills in persons who had, or did not have, previous opportunities to do so. There has been some preliminary work which shows that older persons are capable of developing musical skills well into their 80's provided they have the appropriate opportunities to do so. There has been no research, however, of the effects of this skill development on self-esteem and self-efficacy.

Proposed Study #2: "Music activities as a venue for increasing volunteerism and community involvement in older adults."

Many older adults have music training and abilities that would be beneficial to others. If the older adult chose to volunteer or participate in community music activities, it is theorized that self-esteem would be increased and quality of life improved. A program would be coordinated by a music therapist to identify musical abilities of older adults and refer them to an appropriate volunteer or community participation site. Since older adults are often on a fixed income, minimal funding for transportation or support resources would be necessary for some participants. Effects studied would be contact/participation hours, life satisfaction, and community benefit.

Proposed Study #3: "The effect of music in counseling those who are bereaved or depressed due to the death of a loved one, trauma or personal injury or terminal illness."

Music interventions have been shown to be effective in facilitating counseling relationships and objectives. (Butler, 1966; Stratton and Zalanowsky, 1984). Older adults often are severely depressed or grieving due to a traumatic event in their lives. Research would test the ability of music therapy interventions and counseling techniques to relieve depression, increase interest in social relationships, and provide a structure for the resolution of grief.

<u>Proposed Study #4</u>: "The effect of music-based life review on life satisfaction of institutionalized older adults."

There is a need to evaluate the effectiveness of music-based life review programs in promoting life satisfaction of institutionalized older adults. There is some research that has shown life review programs using music as the primary stimulus to be more effective in increasing life satisfaction over verbal life review programs. In addition, there is evidence to suggest that even the most severely disabled individuals, those who have lost short-term memory capabilities, are able to participate successfully in life review programs that access long-term memory.

<u>Proposed Study #5</u>: "An examination of attitudes toward older mentally retarded members of a community chorus."

While the number of mentally retarded individuals who reach old age is increasing, their support systems in most cases are decreasing. Whether living in group homes, with family members or in institutional facilities, membership in a community organization may be a viable means of broadening their support base and involving them with other older adults. Information concerning the suitability of this kind of mainstreaming is necessary, especially as it relates to community attitude toward mentally retarded older adults.

<u>Proposed Study #6</u>: "The effects of aging on musical performance skills in mentally retarded older adults."

Increases in the number of mentally retarded individuals living in group homes in the community have not resulted in increases in socialization opportunities for these individuals. Community music organizations generally require higher musical performance skills than many mentally retarded individuals are capable of attaining. Research aimed at identifying performance skill levels, and educational capabilities of these individuals, as well as the effects of aging on these two areas is vital to their successful participation in the community.

RESEARCH AREA SEVEN

The Effect of Music on Disease Prevention and General Health of Older Adults

<u>Proposed Study #1</u>: "The effect of background music during mealtime on caloric and nutritional intake of older adults."

Prior research has shown that adults listening to music during weight loss programs consume fewer calories. It is theorized that music may reduce anxiety and create a more leisurely environment, the individual may then eat slower and have time to achieve a replete sensation before consuming a large number of calories. The relationship between music, socialization, and the motivation to eat or feed oneself could be investigated with subjects who are no longer consuming nutritionally balanced diets, who are socially isolated during meals, or who have lost the will to consume food.

<u>Proposed Study #2</u>: "The effect of music and music therapy interventions on endurance, motivation, and physical benefit in exercise programs for older adults."

Exercise prolongs life and maintains wellness, independence and mobility in older adults. Research has suggested that music would increase endurance, motivation, and social interaction during exercise programs. This study would determine the actual effect of the music interventions on these factors and help to identify specific music and musical factors that create the desired effects.

<u>Proposed Study #3</u>: "Music therapy interventions as a motivator in improving the fitness levels of older adults."

Music is effective as a motivator. This quality of music is invaluable in making unpleasant tasks, such as exercise, more pleasant and thus more motivating. Documentation of music and exercise programs with older adults, both in the community and in long-term care facilities is needed.

<u>Proposed Study #4</u>: "Effects of musical task completion on perceived locus of control."

Accepting responsibility for one's actions and future are generally regarded as indicators of good mental health. Musical tasks are structured to allow for personal choices at many different skill levels. Research is warranted to examine the effects of older adults' locus of control as it relates to participation in specific music tasks.

<u>Proposed Study #5</u>: "Intergenerational music programs to maintain vitality and facilitate relationships across the generations."

Intergenerational activities are beginning to attract attention as a way to form bonds and unite the generations. Music therapy strategies provide a creative way to institute this positive, shared experience. Research on the psychological and social impact of music on individuals from all generations will help determine the efficacy of these methods.

REFERENCES

Butler, B. (1966). Music group psychotherapy. <u>Journal of Music Therapy, 3,</u> 53-56.

Clair, A.A. and Bernstein, B. (1990). A comparison of singing, vibrotactile and nonvibrotactile instrumental playing responses in severely regressed persons with dementia of the Alzheimer's type. <u>Journal of Music Therapy, 9</u>(3), 299-311.

Curtis, S.L. (1978). The effects of music on the perceived degree of pain relief, physical comfort, relaxation, and contentment of hospitalized terminally ill patients. Unpublished Master's theses, Florida State University.

Gates, A. and Bradshaw, J. (1977). The role of the cerebral hemispheres in music. <u>Brain and Language, 4,</u> 403-431.

Gfeller, K.E. (1983). Musical mnemonics as an aid to retention with normal and learning disabled students. <u>Journal of Music Therapy, 20,</u> 179-189.

Gould, W. and Okamura, H. (1973). Static lung volumes in singers. <u>Annals of Otolaryngology, 82,</u> 89-95.

Hanser, S.B. (1985). Music therapy and stress reduction research. <u>Journal of Music Therapy, 22,</u> 193-206.

Lucia, C. (1987). Toward developing a model of music therapy intervention in the rehabilitation of head trauma patients. <u>Music Therapy Perspectives, 4,</u> 34-39.

Millard, K.A. and Smith, J.M. (1989). The influence of group singing therapy on the behavior of Alzheimer's disease patients. <u>Journal of Music Therapy, 26,</u> 58-70.

Norberg, A., Melin, E., and Asplund, K. (1986). Reactions to music, touch, and object presentation in the final stage of dementia: An exploratory study. <u>Journal of Music Therapy, 23,</u> 315-323.

Redenbaugh, E.M. (1988). The use of music therapy in developing a communications system in a withdrawn, depressed older adult resident: A case study. <u>Music Therapy Perspectives, 5,</u> 82-83.

Scartelli, J. (1984). The effect of EMG biofeedback and sedative music, EMG biofeedback only, and sedative music only on frontalis muscle relaxation ability. <u>Journal of Music Therapy, 23,</u> 157-165.

Staum, M.J. (1983). Music and rhythmic stimuli in the rehabilitation of gait disorders. <u>Journal of Music Therapy, 20</u>(2), 69-87.

Stratten, V.N. and Zalanowski, A. (1984). The effect of background music on verbal interaction in groups. <u>Journal of Music Therapy, 21,</u> 16-26.

Thaut, M.H. (1991). Musical/rhythmic stimulation as neurological techniques. Paper presented at the 3rd International Conference of Biology of Music Making: Music, Growth, and Aging, Rochester, New York.

Wolfe, D. (1978). Pain rehabilitation and music. <u>Journal of Music Therapy, 15,</u> 162-178.

Senator REID. Your full statement will be made part of the record.

We'll now hear from Dr. Lee.

STATEMENT OF MATHEW LEE, M.D., NEW YORK, NY

Dr. LEE. Senator Reid and Senator Cohen and Senator Pryor, I am grateful for this opportunity to testify this morning concerning the relationships of music, medicine, and rehabilitation medicine.

Currently I serve as Professor and Acting Chairman of the Rusk Institute of Rehabilitation Medicine, New York University; and also as Adjunct Professor of Music. Recently I edited a book entitled, "Rehabilitation, Music, and Human Well-being." The late Howard A. Rusk, in his preface to this book, wrote, "To rehabilitation medicine, it adds a new and vibrant dimension, and to patients, a holistic approach to care."

Anecdotal evidence and personal, clinical experience acknowledge the major role music and the creative art therapies plays in the healing process.

What is exciting today is that we have methods that can measure the physiological and the biochemical effects of music. For example, at New York University it appears that through magnetic imaging we have located an area of the brain which deals with singing, separate from the speech center.

We note that patients, when you play music that they like, will have endorphin levels increased. That perhaps explains why there is pain abatement. Also, if one needs surgery and we play the music that they enjoy pre-, during, and post-surgery, one would require less pain medications and less anesthesia.

As documented, falls, respiratory problems, physical rehabilitation, and chronic pain of the elderly impact greatly on medical costs. Cost containment and cost-effectiveness are major issues.

I strongly believe that with current methodologies and technologies in music we can—one, maintain functional independence at home; two, preclude and prevent hospitalization and, if hospitalized, to reduce stay, in addition to decreasing drug utilization and to improve cognition in our elderly and young.

To achieve the above so that music can be a part of the mainstream of medicine, systematic research through demonstration projects, basic research, and certainly clinical outcome research must be done.

Current attitudes concerning the elderly serve to set minimal levels of aspirations, although the overwhelming evidence clearly indicates that this view is wrong, that this view is unfair, and contrary to the facts.

Music and music therapy enhance the functional capabilities of the elderly, as well as to raise their level of aspiration and potential to more realistic levels.

I cannot think of anyone who could more eloquently articulate the role that music plays than my friend and your colleague, the late Senator Jacob Javitz. In his keynote address during the Fourth International Symposium of Music and Rehabilitation—which was to be his last public appearance—he states, "This is a unique therapy and is a great boon to the disabled, as it should be, and it must be seriously undertaken as an element of medicine."

I thank the Committee for inviting me to testify today.

[The prepared statement of Dr. Lee follows:]

UNITED STATES SENATE

HEARING OF THE SPECIAL COMMITTEE ON AGING

Forever Young: Music and Aging

AUGUST 1, 1991

<u>EXPERT PANEL</u>

MATHEW H.M. LEE, MD, MPH, FACP

Professor and Acting Chairman
Rusk Institute of Rehabilitation Medicine
New York University Medical Center

Professor of Clinical Rehabilitation Medicine
New York University School of Medicine

Adjunct Professor, Department of Music and Music Professions
New York University
School of Education, Health, Nursing and Arts Professions

Clinical Professor of Behavioral Sciences and Community Health
New York University College of Dentistry

Senior Vice President
MedArt USA, Inc.

Prepared with the assistance of:

Fadi J. Bejjani, MD, PhD, Adjunct Professor and Director, Human Performance Analysis Laboratory, Department of Music and Music Professions; Associate Director of Research, Rusk Institute of Rehabilitation Medicine, New York University School of Medicine

Joseph C. Nagler, MA, CMT, Chairman, Research and Development Committee, MedArt USA, Inc.

Herbert Zaretsky, PhD, Administrator, Department of Rehabilitation Medicine, New York University Medical Center

America is getting greyer. By the year 2010, with the maturation of baby boomers, the population of older Americans is projected to rise dramatically. Older Americans as a group have lower economic status than other adults in our society. This largely results from changes in status and loss of earnings associated with aging. More than in any other age group, cost reduction and cost effectiveness are vital issues here.

While acute health problems were predominant at the beginning of the century, chronic conditions are now the more prevalent health problem for the elderly. In the main, these conditions can be prevented, or at least their process slowed a great deal. In 1985, approximately 5.2 million Americans 65 or older were mildly-to-severely disabled and needed assistive technology and special aids to maintain their independence. This figure is expected to reach 7.3 million by the year 2000. These demographic data cannot but result in a growing demand for specialized health care for the elderly, with emphasis on prevention and non-invasive long-term therapies.

Indeed, a particularity of the field of geriatrics is that it requires a team of health care providers who work as a team in a large array of settings — not only in the hospital, but in the home as well. There is, to date, grossly inadequate training and education in the field of geriatrics in this country. This is often compensated for by trained non-medical allied health personnel.

Although rehabilitation technology has been widely used and attempts to alleviate the adverse effects of disability, it has not generally been focused on solving the problems of elderly disabled individuals. Studies show that no more than half of them use their prescribed aids. Frailty and lack of muscle strength render it more difficult to provide adequate aids to this group. Many more factors of a behavioral, psychosocial and emotional nature also come into play: the slower pace of learning, requiring far more repetitions that could be perceived as tedious; the frequent decrease in self-esteem and life satisfaction; an increase in negative outlook on life and self-ageism. Therapy has been clinically found to be most helpful in alleviating these factors and reversing their trend. Rendering assistive technology more interactive with frequent audiovisual feedback is a real breakthrough in this effect.

Orthopedic surgical patients over age 65, primarily with hip fractures, while only 34.5% of total hospital admissions, generate 50% of total hospital costs. The cost in direct care for hip fractures is $7 billion or more per year. Falls are the most important determinant of fracture risk. There is a plethora of factors that may lead to falls, the most important being slower reaction time, decreased balance, and decreased proprioception and coordination. These factors have been proven very responsive to music therapy interventions such as rhythmic auditory stimuli, stimulation of synchronous movement patterns through music, etc.

It is common knowledge that the use of exercise in the elderly is an important factor in the maintenance of health: "Exercise may not add years to their lives, but it can add life to their years." In 1985, a national health survey found that regular appropriate exercise is uncommon among persons age = >65 years. Indeed, exercising can be both tedious and painful, resulting in the withdrawal of many elderly from such routines. Music was found beneficial in distracting their attention and raising their threshold to pain, thereby making repetitive therapeutic movements more meaningful and acceptable to them.

New York University has maintained a strong commitment to music therapy over three decades, most evident in the close alliance that exists between the music therapy program and the Medical Center. The Howard A. Rusk Institute of Rehabilitation Medicine, an integral component of NYU Medical Center, is the world's first facility devoted entirely to rehabilitation medicine, and has served as a model for rehabilitation centers throughout the country and the world. The therapeutic recreation staff, numbering more than 15, serve as faculty for comprehensive music therapy clinical internships.

Current research projects at the Rusk Institute include exploration into the psychodynamic elements of the music therapy process, as well as the creation of a music-based modular computer network aiming to promote independence in the elderly population, prevent the occurrence of falls, and maintain physical and mental fitness.

The author has pioneered in the introduction of diagnostic medical tools such as biofeedback and thermography for music therapy clinicians, enhancing their ability to perform objective measurements and research. He established the first center for the use of computer-music systems in the music therapy process at Goldwater Memorial Hospital. He also has collaborated to sponsor three precedent-setting conferences in this field spanning a ten-year period, and is now co-organizing *MedArt International's First World Congress on Arts and Medicine*, to be held in New York City February 26-March 1, 1992.

Although clinical experience and many anecdotal and sporadic studies all confirm the benefits of music therapy in preventing potentially fatal conditions, enhancing patients' well-being, shortening their hospital stay and increasing their independence thereafter, many longitudinal double-blind controlled studies are now necessary to produce scientific evidence. This task is nowadays greatly enhanced by the availability of objective measurement tools.

It is our opinion that a significant effort should be made at the level of the federal government to encourage research in this area. As America becomes greyer, this research will affect an ever-growing number of its citizens. In these days of economic hardship and escalating health care costs, the search for alternative non-invasive and less costly therapies should be a necessary focus of legislators.

RFPs based on the priority area of "therapeutic effects of music and the creative arts therapies" are long overdue. Sufficient evidence has been gathered through pilot- and case studies to warrant such a step. More than 100 music therapists nationwide have obtained a Ph.D. degree and are fully trained in scholarly and academic research, and should be encouraged to pursue a career in this field. Upon publication of the first such RFP in the Federal Register, no doubt a large number of competitive research grant proposals will be submitted, thus corroborating the above.

Planning should be undertaken towards the establishment of a Center for Music in Medicine, as part of the National Institute on Aging or the National Institute of Child Health and Development, with its own separate funding appropriation. The staff of the Rusk Institute would be honored to serve as part of the planning committee.

A.   BACKGROUND

1.   The Greying of America

During the last two decades, the number of Americans age 65 and older has increased by 56%, compared to an increase of only 19% for the under-65 population (Melcher et al., 1987-1988). Since 1980, an average of 168,000 persons per month marked their 65th birthday. At the beginning of this century, less than 1 in 10 Americans was 55 and over and 1 in 25 was 65 and over. By 1986, 1 in 5 Americans was at least 55 years old and 1 in 8 was at least 65. Between 1985 and 2050, the total U.S. population is projected to increase by 33%, while this increase will be 200% for the 55 plus population. By 2010, with the maturation of baby boomers, the population of older Americans is projected to rise dramatically; 1 in 4 of the total population will be at least 55, and 1 in 7 will be at least 65 years old.

The elderly population is also growing older. In 1986, 41% of this population was age 75 and older. It is projected that by the year 2000, 50% will be 75-plus. According to the 1980 census, there are 3.2 million people in New York State who are 60 or older. More than a million reside in the New York metropolitan area. Today, individuals over age 75 comprise the fastest growing segment of the population. The disability rate in this age group is 8 times greater than that of the under-45 age group. In addition, older persons are much more likely to have multiple chronic illnesses and more severe disabilities. More than 40 percent of all disabled persons in the United States are over age sixty (Kemp et al., 1989).

Today the non-white and Hispanic populations have a smaller proportion of elderly than the white. In 1986, 13% of whites were 65 or over, compared to only 8% of non-whites and 5% of Hispanics. The difference is a result of higher fertility for the non-white and Hispanic populations. These proportions are expected to remain relatively stable during the next two decades. In the early part of the next century, however, the proportion of elderly is expected to increase at a higher rate for the non-white (265%) and the Hispanic (530%) populations, than for the white population (97%) (Melcher et al.).

Older Americans, as a group, have a lower economic status than other adults in our society. This largely results from changes in status often associated with aging. In retirement, elderly persons lose earnings and become reliant instead upon social security benefits supplemented with pensions and the assets they have accumulated over their lifetimes. With limited potential to improve their income through work, older persons become economically vulnerable to circumstances over which they have no control: the loss of a spouse, deterioration of their health and self-sufficiency, social security and Medicare legislation, and inflation. Compared strictly on the basis of monetary income, persons 65 and older, on average, receive substantially less income than those under 65. In 1986, the median income of families with heads age 65 or older was $19,932, about 62% of the median income of families with heads age 25 to 64 ($32,368). In the same year, 12.4% of persons 65 and older had incomes below the poverty level, compared to 10.8% of those age 18 to 64. The oldest among the elderly (85 plus) have significantly lower monetary incomes than those who are 65 to 84 years (Melcher et al.).

Black and Hispanic elderly have substantially lower monetary incomes than their white counterparts. In 1986, the median income of black males age 65 plus ($6,757) was 56% of white males ($12,131) and that of Hispanic males of the same age ($7,369) was 61% of white males. Black and Hispanic women also had lower median incomes than their white counterparts. The median income of black women age 65 plus ($4,508) was 67% of white women ($6,738); that of Hispanic women of the same age ($4,583) was 68% of white women (Melcher et al.).

While acute health problems were predominant at the beginning of the century, chronic conditions are now the more prevalent health problem for the elderly. The likelihood of suffering from a chronic disease or disabling condition increases with age. Seventy five percent of strokes occur after age 65. Most amputations occur in elderly persons. The majority of hip fractures occur in people between the ages of 70 to 78 years. Eighty-six percent of the elderly population over 65 develop at least one chronic condition and 52 percent of those over 75 have some limitations in the conduct of their daily activities (Kemp et al., 1989). In 1986, the leading chronic conditions among the elderly were arthritis, hypertension, hearing impairments and heart disease. The likelihood of suffering from arthritis is 68% higher for those 65 and older than for those 45 to 64.

In 1985, approximately 5.2 million Americans 65 or older were mildly-to-severely disabled and needed assistance and special aids to maintain their independence. This figure is expected to reach 7.3 million by the year 2000. Disability in the elderly is commonly measured according to the degree of difficulty experienced in performing activities of daily living (ADL), i.e. personal care and home management. About 25% of the persons 65 and older living in the community (95% of all the 65 plus population) have difficulty with one or more of the seven personal care activities inventoried (bathing, dressing, eating, getting in and out of bed/chairs, walking, going outside, using the toilet). About the same proportion experienced difficulty with at least one of the six home management activities (preparing meals, shopping for personal items, managing money, using the telephone, doing heavy housework, doing light housework). This proportion increased with age, rising from 15%, for those age 65-69, to 49% for those 85 and over (Melcher et al., 1987-1988).

These demographic data cannot but result in a growing demand for specialized health care for the elderly. However, despite this growing demand for geriatricians, the field has difficulty attracting physicians because of the inequities of the Medicare reimbursement system and because providing general care to an elderly patient is deemed less prestigious than other specialties such as cardiology (Monahan, 1988). Another particularity of the field of geriatrics is that it requires a team of health providers, including music therapists, who work together to take care of older people in a larger array of settings, not only in the hospital but in the home (Monahan). Perhaps the most eloquent proof of concerned interests in this topic are two articles that appeared in the New York Times Health section. The first voiced some relief: "Finally, doctors ask if brutal falls need be a fact of life in the elderly" (Thursday 12/29/1988, p. B9). After exposing some hard facts and reviewing the state-of-the-art, it is clearly stated that, although engaged, the struggle is not over yet and a great deal remains to be done. The other article published excerpts of a report, written by the Inspector General of the Department of Health and Human and Services (DHHS), related to the "wide medication misuse in the elderly." He found that 51% of deaths from drug reactions occur in people age 60 and older, even though they account for only 17% of the population. Misdiagnoses by doctors and faulty prescribing were incriminated and primarily attributed to inadequate medical training and education in geriatrics (Wednesday 2/13/1989, pp. A1, A17). Perhaps the most concerning problem in the elderly is drug intake, as a stand alone or because of its relationship to falls. It has been called "the nation's other drug problem." Williamson (1978) noted that 87% of those individuals over 75 years old living in the community were on medication, with 34% taking 3 or 4 different drugs. Hamdy et al. (1977) found that two thirds of apparently fit old people living at home had at least one illness. On average, each hospitalized elderly patient has six diseases. Multiple pathology leads to polypharmacy, which seems to be the rule in this population. In 1967, nearly three times as many prescriptions were given to American patients over 65 (11.4 per person) as were given to those under 65 (4.0 per person) (Task Force on Prescription Drugs, 1968). In 1977, 39% of prescriptions for hypnotics were for patients 60-plus, and over half the prescriptions for barbiturates were for this age group.

Another very important aspect of the geriatric population's needs is housing. Although it becomes increasingly difficult with advancing age, the vast majority of older people (84 percent) wish to remain in their present home with familiar surroundings, never having to leave it (AARP survey, 1990). The New York State office on the aging has determined that, in recent years, advancements in technological and architectural design features have made it possible to design housing that will accommodate the gradually changing needs that many individuals experience during the normal aging process. Adaptive technology, incorporated unobtrusively into housing units, can maintain a continuing balance for older residents. Recent advances in technology have led to the feasibility of designing low cost systems that can aid older citizens in accomplishing daily living activities. Several studies have recently investigated new technologies to assist elderly and disabled individuals in the home setting (Potman 1980; Prosper, 1990; Trimble, 1989). Increasing attention is being paid to personal computer based systems that will allow unrestricted access to essential services previously beyond the reach of individuals whose mobility has significantly deteriorated with age. Since 1984, both industry and government (through the Office of Special Education and Rehabilitation Services [OSERS] and the National Institute on Disability and Rehabilitation Research [NIDRR]) have supported the provision of computer services to senior citizens and the disabled. Vanderheiden et al. (1989a) have studied various methods of increasing the accessibility of computers and information services to persons with disabilities. A second phase of this study, conducted by Borden (1988), focused on disseminating current information about available products. Other novel projects are underway to promote the standardization of the connections between user-interface devices and the electronic-assist devices used by disabled individuals (Vanderheiden, 1989b).

2.   Needs of the Elderly and Service Providers

Older persons have special needs that are a consequence of the aging process. They are faced with functional limitations very similar to those experienced by people with disabilities acquired through accidents or disease. Medical, neurological, and orthopedic impairments become increasingly common as the age of the population increases. Typical conditions resulting in disability include heart disease, hypertension, stroke, arthritis, hip fractures, Alzheimer's disease, pulmonary disease, and deficits in hearing and vision.

Although rehabilitation technology has been widely used in attempts to alleviate the adverse effects of disability and impairments, it has not generally been focused on solving the problems of elderly disabled individuals. Devices and techniques aimed at ameliorating specific disabilities are usually designed to augment or take advantage of residual compensatory abilities. Therefore, frailty and lack of muscle strength in the elderly population compounds the difficulties and renders it even more difficult to provide adequate aids to this group of individuals. Moreover, it is interesting to note that older persons experiencing problems in performing their activities of daily living, do not, for the most part, consider themselves to be disabled. Because they do not perceive the serious nature of their deficits, they rarely accept the need for adaptive devices and, hence, ignore available assistive technology. For this reason, it is important that technology now be utilized specifically with the problems of the elderly in mind. Efforts must be made to remain sensitive to the general negativity of older individuals to new technological developments and to devise effective ways to introduce new assistive technology to this population. Different dissemination media and service systems must be used to reach older persons.

In a study of 500 elderly individuals who owned assistive devices, Page et al. (1980) found that approximately half of them did not use these aids either because they had been inaccurately prescribed, did not work, were unsafe or broken or because the elderly person considered the disability as a minor inconvenience to be tolerated rather than to be overcome.

Another need of the elderly that will be met by the application of computers is their need for a slower pace of learning and for more repetitions of an activity to strengthen learning. Use of a computer network would allow the elderly to better assimilate desired knowledge by means of repetitive methods of learning.

Mastering computer programs might also serve to ameliorate an age-related social phenomenon known as ageism. Chronological age, in and of itself, is often a major factor influencing a senior citizen's self esteem. Older persons often see themselves as not having a capacity to deal with disability equal to that of a younger person. Additionally, older individuals are less likely to believe that they will be able to recover from a disabling condition and are more likely to believe that they do not have enough time left to adjust (Kemp, 1986).

Childress (1986) has suggested that the most effective use of technology is in the prevention of the need for assistive devices in the first place. Using simple technical aids (auto seat belts, walkers, grab bars and balance aids such as canes) to prevent serious injuries and the resulting disabilities is the most advantageous use of technology in the maintenance of functional independence.

Safety is an important factor in deciding upon the goals of rehabilitation when working with geriatric patients. For example, the concern of a physical therapist working with an older person with a gait disturbance is often centered on the patient's safety. However, for the elderly person, it may be better to walk incorrectly than to not walk at all. Decisions based on safety issues are heavily value-laden. One of the greatest needs of older persons is to remain independent. Many of these individuals fear the loss of independence more than they fear death. They would rather take the risk of falling than be placed in a nursing home (Kemp et al., 1989). In this regard, the extensive use of medications by the elderly may also contribute to problems in maintaining a safe environment.

Disability has a major impact on life satisfaction in the elderly (Kemp et al., 1989). For a person to have life satisfaction, there must be sufficient pleasurable experiences to outweigh whatever painful ones may occur during the course of daily living. A disability increases the source of pain in life without a corresponding increase in pleasure. In later life, a disability is often in addition to other painful losses such as absence of spouse, low vision, decreased hearing and inability to get out and socialize within the community. Other major difficulties presented by a disability include the lack of control over one's life and the loss of a sense of meaning or purpose in life. The topic of life satisfaction after disability is a very important one in the process of rehabilitation. Individuals with low satisfaction will not only lead very unhappy lives but they will also suffer from more medical and psychological disorders and will require more health care and social support than others of the same age (Kemp et al., 1989).

Self-esteem is another personal quality that is severely affected by disability. People who can accept and appreciate themselves after a disability maintain their self-esteem and are able to lead happier, more productive lives than those who no longer see themselves as valuable members of society. One of the major problems with poor self-esteem is that it tends to lead to self perpetuating, destructive behavior such as poor self-care and negative mental attitudes towards their ability to improve physically or to accomplish positive achievements.

3.   Health Problems of the Elderly: Issues in Prevention

Falls

In a series of 1,040 orthopaedic patients (Munoz et al., 1988), those between the ages of 80 and 85, while comprising only 5.5% of total hospital admissions, generated 10% of total hospital costs. Orthopaedic surgical patients over age 65, while only 34.5% of total hospital admissions, generated 50% of total hospital costs. Although mean hospital cost for all patients was $9,345, the mean cost for those 80 and older was $17,858. Total personal health care expenditures for the elderly were $120 billion in 1984, with a per capita spending of $4,200, representing a 13% average annual increase from 1977. Each year, it is estimated, more than 200,000 Americans over the age of 65, suffer hip fractures, and 20,000 to 30,000 of them die of complications. Fewer than 25% of the survivors ever regain their previous mobility. The cost in direct care is $7 billion or more per year (Pokras, 1984). The most important determinants of fracture risk, i.e. hip fracture, are falls and reduced skeletal resistance, i.e. bone loss (Melton et al., 1985).

Falls are only the most dramatic and quantifiable aspect of a larger problem. This problem extends beyond the act of falling to the loss of self-confidence, the fear of its recurrence, and the immobility this produces. This larger aspect limits the lives of far more old people than the actual frequency of their falling. Whether directly or indirectly affected by falls, most old people are aware of the resulting problems. The insecurity this produces may be intangible, but it often has a considerable impact on older people's lives and may have substantial economic repercussions (MacDonald, 1985).

The rate of falls in a nursing home was found to be approximately 2 per patient per year (Baker et al., 1985). Gryfe et al. (1977) found an annual fall rate of 668 per 1000 among an active ambulatory institutionalized population over 65. As for community-based studies, the reliance on subject recall for documenting falls often results in under-reporting of events and misreporting of circumstances. This explains the wide variability in reported falling rates in the literature: from 24% (Campbell et al., 1981) to 62% (Perry, 1982). With regard to the severity of falls, in a study of 147 falls in a nursing home, Rodstein (1964) found that only 1.4% resulted in major injury. Among 651 falls in a home for the aged, Ashley et al. (1977) found 17.5% caused major injury. Fall-associated mortality is the seventh leading cause of death in persons 75 and older (Ochs et al., 1985). The mortality rate rises exponentially with age, ranging from 37/100,000 in those 75 to 79 years, to 186/100,000 in persons 85 years and older (Pokras, 1984). In females, between age periods 65 to 74 and 75 to 84, the death rate from falls increases fivefold, while the injury rate only increases twofold. The ratio of fall deaths to injuries more than doubles (Baker et al., 1985).

There is a plethora of factors that may lead to falls and may also contribute to related functional deficits such as slow gait and inability to climb stairs. Falls are only the tip of an iceberg that encompasses these less-dramatic but widespread problems.

Although some gait alterations in the elderly are controversial, e.g. inability (Hurwitz, 1968) versus ability (Potvin et al., 1980) to walk tandem, there seems to be a general consensus on the following clinical characteristics of senile gait: wide-base; poor truncal stability; gait dysrhythmia; flexed posture; shortened steps; bradykinesia; loss of associated arm movements; and gait apraxia. Imms et al. (1981) reported that walking speed diminishes with age and is accompanied by diminished stride length, step frequency, and swing/stance phase time. Walking speed is also dependent upon an individual's habitual level of activity with independently functioning individuals walking faster than those who are housebound. Gait of "fallers" is even more compromised than the normal elderly, with decreased walking speed, shorter stride length, as well as a variability in the length of progressive steps (Guimaraes, et al. 1980). The presence of irregular interjected steps (staggering) seems highly characteristic, even predictive, of fallers (Wolfson et al., 1985).

Many studies reported an increase of sway (unsteadiness) as persons age, and retrospectively associated the amount of sway with a history of falling (Brocklehurst et al., 1982; Imms, et al. 1981; Kirshen et al., 1984; Overstall et al., 1977, 1978). Fernie et al. (1982) found an increased sway in fallers that did not correlate with the number of falls. Although sway has been amply correlated with falling, the nature of this relationship has not been defined, nor has the relationship of this static measure of balance to the more dynamic balance required to make the rapid adjustment of the lower extremities and center of gravity to prevent falls.

In healthy individuals in their 60's and 70's, there is a 20% to 40% decrease of isometric strength in all muscles tested, both proximal and distal. There is a 38% decrement of strength from the third through seventh decades, which is most prominent at higher speeds of contraction. This has been related to atrophy of the fast twitch (Type II) muscle fiber (Larsson et al., 1979). Wolfson et al. (1985) found severely compromised motor function, well out of range of what is seen in normal aging, in specific lower extremity muscles of individuals who fall. Ankle muscles had particularly poor function (10% of control values). Unbalanced strength of the muscles acting about the ankle has been indicated as a prominent cause of injury.

Abnormalities of proprioception have been noted in 15 to 40% of elderly patients, depending on the series (Kokmen et al., 1978; Wolfson et al., 1985). Quantitative determination of proprioception at the knee reveals a deterioration with age that might make walking unsafe or impossible (Skinner et al. 1984). Vibration sense decreases significantly after 50 years, primarily in the lower extremities (Steiness 1957), and results in a two- to tenfold decrease in the perceptual threshold (Perret et al., 1970; Potvin et al. 1980). Rabinowitz (1982) found astereognosis of the sole of the foot after age 60 in 20% of subjects with normal gait. This proportion raised to 80% in subjects with gait abnormalities.

Virtually all studies agree that the general effect of taking drugs is to increase fall frequency in the elderly. Prudham et al. (1981) showed that 48% of a large stratified population sample of individuals over age 65 taking any drug had fallen in the past year. The figure was only 42% for non-users of drugs. Davie et al. (1981), in a psychogeriatric outpatient population, found that any drug increased the incidence of dizziness or falling. MacDonald (1985) reports that virtually every femoral fracture occurring at night (93%) was in a person taking barbiturates. In 1,622 geriatric outpatients, 85% of patients taking barbiturates were referred for falls or dizziness; whereas only 24% of the referrals were not taking barbiturates. Wild et al. (1981) noted that 9 of 11 elderly fallers in the community who had severe postural hypotension, and were prone to falling, were taking antihypertensive drugs or drugs with a hypotensive action.

Mossey (1985) thoroughly reviewed the literature concerning social and psychologic factors related to falls. The presence of acute and/or chronic illness and functional impairment are the most consistent factors observed to be related to falls and serious fall-related injuries. Prudham et al.'s (1981) study of self-reported falls in community-dwelling residents reported 9% of the fallers to have a major problem with cognitive function as compared to 6.1% of the non-fallers.

Environmental factors play a large role in the occurrence of falls. Tideiksaar (1990) found the majority of the falls occur in the bedroom and kitchen and on the stairway. He concludes that 72% of the participants in the study experienced a decrease in the number of falls after the environmental changes were introduced.

Physical Activity and Exercise

In a very recent study on 50 elderly women, Lichtenstein et al. (1989) concluded that controlled clinical trials to study the effect of physical therapy and exercise on balance measures in community-dwelling elderly women are feasible. The exercise program in this study was designed with the intent of improving balance, flexibility, and reaction time. It consisted of a combination of stretching, active and static balance, response exercises and walking, lasting a total of 60 minutes per session. Each subject had 48 sessions, at the rate of 3 sessions per week. The effect of exercise was determined by the sole measurement of sway on a force platform, before and after. Exercise effect was found inconsistent due to several factors, including lack of compliance, lack of statistical power, ineffective and inadequate duration of the exercise program, etc. Benefits of cardiovascular exercise in old age has also been described (Gorman et al., 1988). Spirduso (1975, 1980) found that reaction time in older exercisers was similar to that of younger subjects and significantly faster than the age-matched sedentary men.

Titiloye's (1988) study in occupational therapy documented the relationship of age to reaction time and movement time of a functional self-paced task in healthy adult females. Normative data of the decline in the central nervous systems' capacity to process self-paced functional task of drinking from a cup in well elderly were obtained. The results indicate that deteriorative effect of aging may not be limited to speeded activities but may include self-paced tasks as well. Titiloye has disseminated the results of her study to practicing occupational therapists, occupational therapy students, other health professionals, and the older adults who participated in the study. Also in the realm of occupational therapy, mobility requiring balance maneuvers, namely rising from a chair, turning and prolonged standing were identified as good predictors of recurrent falling (Tinetti et al., 1981; Tobis et al., 1981). It has also been indicated that more falls occur when the older patient is distracted by manipulating or holding an object, or performing an activity (Overstall et al., 1981).

Stodefalke (1985) reports the differences in motivating an elderly person to exercise stem from the approaches taken when introducing and implementing the program. He stratifies the approaches into two categories: mechanistic and humanistic. He states that although the study of exercise is a science, the leading of exercise is an art. In comparing the approaches to exercise in the Table below, it is apparent that the mechanistic approach towards exercise differs greatly from the humanistic. The intrinsic motivation of the humanistic approach appears to be well suited for this population.

COMPARISON OF MECHANISTIC AND HUMANISTIC APPROACHES TO EXERCISE

	Mechanistic approach	Humanistic approach
Emphasis	Organization, *process* and participant safety	Organization, *person* and participant safety
Goal	To improve participant's cardiorespiratory function, range of motion, and muscular strength and endurance	To encourage continued physical activity in an unsupervised environment based on a foundation of education and enjoyment
Definition of physical activity	A treatment prescribed for restoration and improvement of heart and circulatory function, flexibility, and muscular strength and endurance	A physical expression elected to improve heart and circulatory system function, flexibility, and muscular strength and endurance
Elements of exercise regimen	Well-defined types of activity, intensity of energy expenditure, duration of each activity session, and frequency of an exercise stimulus	Although well defined, permit some freedom of choice in selection and conduct of activities
Organization	Elaborate flow charts for entrance and exit criteria, educational seminars, and reporting systems	Participant involvement in goal setting, education, and reward systems

The use of exercise in the elderly is an important factor in the maintenance of health. Millar (1987) found that a simple exercise program for the older person that is not stressful and does no harm, could yield a good rate of compliance (> 70%). It is a program aimed at making the patient feel better, whether or not there is a measurable improvement in cardiorespiratory function. Smith and Gilligan (1983) report that disuse accounts for almost half of the functional decline in persons between 30 and 70 years of age. They maintain that this trend can be changed with a well-planned physical activity program.

Simple exercise routines such as "jarming" (jogging with the arms) and natural calisthenics (Simpson, 1986; DeVries, 1971) can lead to longevity. Elkowitz & Elkowitz (1986) found that "Exercise may not add years to peoples lives, but it can add life to their years." (p.91). They also state that the exercise potential of many older persons can be assessed and their maximal heart rate determined without elaborate equipment.

Regular physical activity and exercise are critical elements in adult health promotion. Increased levels of physical activity are associated with a reduced incidence of coronary heart disease (Powell et al., 1987), hypertension (Paffenbarger et al., 1983), noninsulin-dependent diabetes mellitus 1985), reduces the risk for osteoporotic fractures (Cooper et al., 1988), helps maintain appropriate body weight (Blair et al., 1985), and increases longevity (Paffenbarger et al., 1986).

Analysis of the 1985 National Health Interview Survey supplemental questionnaire on health promotion and disease prevention found that regular, appropriate exercise is uncommon among persons aged greater than or equal to 65 years. Only 7%-8% of this age group regularly engage in exercise capable of maintaining or improving cardiorespiratory fitness (CDC, 1989). Moreover, about two thirds of persons in this age group are either active irregularly or completely sedentary. The remainder exercise regularly but at an intensity too low to improve their cardiorespiratory fitness (Caspersen et al., 1985).

4. Music Therapy and the Elderly

Music therapy is a form of treatment in which the patient and therapist are involved in an interactive musical dialogue that is designed to help foster the rehabilitation of the patient (Nordoff and Robbins, 1977). In the music therapy process, music is the medium and the means of communication (Nordoff and Robbins, 1983).

Music therapy has proven to be an effective medium for patients with severe physical problems (Cook 1986); Davis-Rollans and Cunningham, 1987 Nagler and Lee, 1987). The literature of music therapy is rich with sources that have demonstrated this modality to be an effective form of therapy in treating the geriatric patient (Gilbert 1977), (Glynn 1986), (Milligan 1986), (Palmer 1977), (Smith 1986), (Wolfe 1983). There have been several studies using traditional music therapy techniques that have influenced the formation of the theoretical framework of this proposed study that illustrate the efficacy of this treatment (Bonny 1983), (Bailey 1985), (Staum 1983).

Additionally, in music therapy, Tomaino (1979) noted that one significant aging process in the elderly is a decrease in the ability to move through space (Phillips 1980). Coordination of movement is enhanced through the use of music. In particular, rhythm acts as an external organizer to stimulate synchronous movement patterns (Tomaino 1979). Straum (1983) found that the application of rhythmic auditory stimuli as a superimposed structure in facilitating proprioceptive control of rhythmic gait was most effective in patients with hemiparesis secondary to stroke, spastic disorders, and painful arthritic or scoliotic conditions. Frequently, elderly persons must be involved in extensive exercises to maintain and/or re-establish optimal movement. Such exercises can be both tedious and painful, resulting in the withdrawal of many elderly from such routines. Music can be used to distract their attention and to raise their threshold to pain thereby making repetitive movements more meaningful and acceptable (Bright 1972). New research in the field of psychoneuroimmunology suggests that the production of morphine-like peptides or endorphins, likely to increase pain tolerance, may be connected to certain musical experiences (Bonny 1986).

The use of technology to meet the needs of patients in the music therapy process is a new and emerging trend in this field (Krout 1987a, 1987b, 1988a, 1988b and Obara 1985). Greenfield (1985), Gregory and Sims (1987), and Krout and Mason (1988) have all used this technology as an adjunctive, non-process-based element of the music therapy session.

The use of computer music technology in the music therapy session as a tool for clinical use has been reported by Nagler (1986) and then Nagler and Lee (1989), Salmon and Newmark (1990) and Spitzer

(1989). All of these studies achieved diverse and, at times, contradictory results. One common point that they all express is the use of computer music technology to either teach music or effect a therapeutic change in music therapy session work.

Bioelectrical controllers have been employed in the music therapy process, allowing the body to create sound without the use of traditional instruments (Knapp and Lusted, 1990) (Nagler, 1990). Controllers of this fashion will be of importance to this project in creating new data entry methods for the users of this network.

Recently, clinicians have developed techniques and instruments that have allowed therapists new data for use in the manner they approach their patients (Davis-Rollans and Cunningham, 1987; Gregory and Sims, 1987). Preliminary studies have shown that the incorporation of music life review techniques (Vanderark, Newman and Bell, 1983) can prove beneficial in aiding the patient in resolution of many psychosocial issues (Bennett and Mass, 1988; Hoyt and Creech, 1983).

5. Technological Solutions for the Elderly Disabled

Computers can provide new opportunities for many people (Scripp, Meyaard, Davidson, 1988). Current computer technology can provide an effective means of delivering health care towards rehabilitation for the geriatric patient (Furlong and Kearsley, 1986). Yet, the scope of the services that technology can provide is hampered by the effectiveness of this modality because of two mitigating factors. The first factor is the inappropriateness of many technological devices in regard to this population's unique needs (Greenfield, 1985; McDonald and Schvaneveldt, 1988). This, coupled with the lack of familiarity of many older people with technology, can render even well-designed devices useless (Laurel, 1990; Maass, 1983).

The second factor associated with the ineffective use of technology for this population is the difficult learning curve that is present for the geriatric person when attempting to assimilate this technology into their daily routines (McGuire, 1986). Many older people who suffer from disabilities have several distinct and unique problems (Williams 1986; Rubenfeld, 1986).

The conditions that can lead to these factors can be summarized as follows:

- Slower integration of information and stimuli. Often, an elderly person will require more repetition of the information that is presented.
- A negative outlook on life often accompanying an aging person. Self-ageism is pervasive, for the elderly view their capacity and skills as a diminishing commodity. As an elderly person becomes engrossed in this negativity, often times their self-image is deeply affected.
- Life satisfaction diminishes along with social interaction causing isolation and withdrawal to permeate many areas of their daily existence.
- A lack of patient interest and motivation in following the prescribed rehabilitation program.
- A lack of appropriate tools to stimulate a patient into becoming an active participant in his/her rehabilitation.
- The inability to provide adequate data for clinical analysis of the patient's rehabilitation process.

A rather common task could take on a new dimension when attempted by a person of advanced years. Diminished capacity, visual and hearing impediments, as well as reduced cognitive abilities can render even the simplest of technologies useless. All of these factors can play a significant role in some people's lack of ability to operate and maintain fully functional lives with a degree of happiness and a sense of self worth. The use of video games and other related activities can lead to an increased level of self esteem and an enjoyable learning experience (Weisman, 1983).

Senior citizens with disabilities are in a need of technology which will improve their lives while helping to negate the factors described earlier. Technology that will enjoy successful interaction with elderly people will need to be devoid of a sharp learning curve (Nagler and Lee 1989). The technology must allow the user immediate and total control of the device and still remain stimulating and powerful enough to engage them on a continuing basis.

Childress (1986) addressed the need for the development of appropriate technologies for the elderly. Yet, he does not define the need for applications that computer technology can render beneficial. He does stipulate, however, that the devices that are presently available to the elderly can be beneficial provided that they are not "too complicated" (p. 307).

Yet, if technology were to be used in a manner that is appropriate to the needs of the elderly disabled person, there would be a multiplicity of rewards. These rewards would not only benefit the elderly person, but society at large. Studies have demonstrated that, as society ages, a larger and more disproportionate burden is placed on society to support this distinct group. One study has found that the problem of mobility in the aging has produced a cost to this country of two billion dollars a year in medical care for hip fractures alone (Williams, 1986). If appropriate care and intervention could be utilized to impel the frail and failing aged person into a state of increased mobility, this cost would diminish.

Technology can play a significant role in assisting this cause. A person's range of motion, functional exercise capacity and cardiovascular fitness can be improved with simple and interesting activities that can be programmed accordingly. The use of creative, novel and stimulating devices will engage rehabilitation patients in purposeful activities that reduce the length of recovery.

An example of a special product to be used by the elderly is a collection of compact disks of music relevant to the patient's life experiences. All of this music can be interactively controlled with user responses to a series of activities designed to improve several areas of the patient's functioning. These areas include the patient's range of motion, cardiovascular fitness, and cognitive skills.

This technology is unique because of its ability to precisely monitor unrefined motion with precision in a cost-effective manner. Rudimentary examples of this technology are available in popular electronic games. This menu item will use two technologies to create data input. They are motion-sensitive pads and motion-sensitive fields.

The introduction of computer music technology to the music therapy process is an exciting application of using computers in the therapeutic process. What at first glance may seem like an unnatural pairing of therapy and science is actually a quite complementary and compelling means of reaching a patient in the therapeutic process. A common perception of this application of technology is that it can be technocratic and devoid of the "warmth" of traditional instruments. It is the author's experience that this is not a true or valid perception. As will be demonstrated later in case studies, a very satisfactory and humanistic experience can be achieved creating music with computer music technology.

The use of computer music technology in the music therapy process arose out of several needs that were facing clinicians at the time of the method's inception. First and foremost was the need to provide the patient with maximum opportunity to express him/herself musically — that is, without limitations of a handicapping condition or a "lack" of musical ability. Just as an "able-bodied" person can create music freely and expressively by striking a drum, so too should a person with diminished physical capacities or an inability to express him/herself in a conventional manner be able to convey his/her musical intensions through interactions on an instrument.

Clinical uses of this technology range from motion analysis to creating data gloves, weighted data gloves, and weights with attached sensors allowing the creation of data. A data glove is a device that contains this technology and is able to create data without the constraints of the two-dimensional field housed in the plastic box. By attaching weights to the glove, or sensors to the actual weights, clinical data is created.

B.   NEW YORK UNIVERSITY'S COMMITMENT TO MUSIC THERAPY AND THE ELDERLY

New York University has maintained a strong commitment to music therapy for over three decades. New York University's music therapy program is part of the School of Education, Health, Nursing and Arts Professions. The program maintains a competency-based curriculum in the Master's and Doctoral levels as mandated by the American Association for Music Therapy.

Students in this program complete a comprehensive course of study which is clinically based. Students are trained in the theories, methods and practices of music therapy. This training includes a broad spectrum of classroom experience, fieldwork and participation in group music therapy that is designed to develop a sense of the elements involved in music therapy practice. The development of music skills and clinical improvisation are fundamental components of this curricula. Before completion of their course of studies, students must complete a one-year internship in a clinical setting to develop and master their skills.

One aspect of this program is the Nordoff and Robbins Music Therapy Clinic. This clinic is under the direction of Clive Robbins. It serves as an advanced training center for clinicians to develop their skills as music therapists working with profoundly handicapped and autistic children.

Another aspect of this program is the close alliance that exists between the music therapy program and the New York University Medical Center. The Medical Center serves as a setting for clinical internships. The Howard A. Rusk Institute of Rehabilitation Medicine has served as the internship site for many music therapy students and continues to sponsor and collaborate in some of the most advanced research being undertaken in the field to date.

The Howard A. Rusk Institute of Rehabilitation Medicine

The Howard A. Rusk Institute of Rehabilitation Medicine, an integral component of New York University Medical Center, is the world's first facility devoted entirely to rehabilitation medicine. Founded in 1948 by Howard A. Rusk, MD, considered the father of rehabilitation medicine, the Rusk Institute is the world's largest university-affiliated center of its kind and has maintained its preeminent position as a superb facility for the rehabilitation and training of adults and children with disabilities, for research into the causes and treatment of a wide range of disabilities, and for the education of rehabilitation professionals.

Accredited by the Commission on Accreditation of Rehabilitation Facilities and the Joint Commission on Accreditation of Healthcare Organizations, the Rusk Institute has served as the model for rehabilitation centers throughout the country and the world.

In addition to setting the standard in rehabilitation medicine, the Rusk Institute has numerous patient care innovations to its credit, including:

- one of the first comprehensive programs for the rehabilitation of patients following spinal cord injury and head trauma;
- the development of technical aids for a variety of disabilities;
- advanced application of biofeedback and video games to retrain the muscles of stroke patients;
- a preschool for inpatients and outpatient infants and toddlers with disabilities;
- the Enid A. Haupt Glass Garden, in which the first hospital-based horticultural therapy is housed;
- education for the disabled driver with specially-equipped cars; and
- Independent Living Experience, housed in a specially-equipped apartment, in preparation for discharge to the community.

Patients from around the world are referred to the Rusk Institute. More than 1,000 inpatients stay at its 152-bed facility annually, and more than 8,000 outpatients a year account for over 65,000 outpatient visits. Patients are treated for a full range of disabilities, including stroke, aphasia, amputation, chronic pain, head and spinal cord injuries, pulmonary diseases, neuromuscular diseases, cerebral palsy, spina bifida and scoliosis.

Treatment is organized around a comprehensive interdisciplinary team approach, with attending physiatrist as the team leader, and including specialists in physical therapy, occupational therapy, nursing, speech pathology, psychology, social work, vocational rehabilitation and therapeutic recreation, as well as clinical specialists from other divisions of NYU Medical Center. Individually-structured programs are designed to meet the daily needs of patients during the hospital stay and after discharge, encouraging family members' involvement in all phases of treatment (see Appendix 1).

Current Research Grants and Projects

Some of the more recent projects include explorations into the psychodynamic elements of the music therapy process and research into the use of computer-music systems with physically-disabled patients. One of the more notable projects involves the work of Dr. Rodolfo L. Llinas. Dr. Llinas is exploring the use of non-invasive functional brain imaging to explore the center in the brain related to music-making and cognition.

Dr. Fadi Bejjani and Joseph Nagler have recently submitted two major research grant proposals: "Technology for Older Persons with Disabilities" (Department of Education, NIDRR) and "National Eldercare Institute on Health Promotion" (DHHS-AOA). Both grants greatly emphasize the use of music and computer technology in a modular software network (Eldernet), aiming to promote independence in the elderly population, prevent the occurrence of falls, and maintain physical and mental fitness.

Dr. Mathew Lee's Commitment to Music Therapy and the Elderly

Dr. Mathew Lee's involvement in the field of music therapy has been acknowledged as both visionary and pioneering. He has been instrumental in the introduction of diagnostic medical tools for music therapy clinicians. He has bridged the gap between the medical and music therapy communities of clinicians (see Appendix 2).

He has done so by using computer-music tools in collaborative medical/music therapy research that are now used for assessment and treatment in music therapy. In a collaborative endeavor with the Center for Electronic Music, Dr. Lee established the first center for the use of computer-music systems in the music therapy process at Goldwater Memorial Hospital in New York City. Dr. Lee has been pivotal in the introduction of both biofeedback and thermography techniques that now show great promise for the next generation of research (see Appendix 3). One such device is capable of using the body's bioelectrical energy to produce real-time sound via MIDI computer-musical-instrument control.

As founding member of Music Education for the Handicapped, he has collaborated to sponsor three precedent-setting conferences spanning a ten-year period (see Appendix 4 A,B). His first, a world congress held in 1981 — *Music Therapy and the Physically Disabled* — is still actively cited in the research literature to date. The second, held in 1985 — *The Fourth International Conference on Music, Rehabilitation and Human Well-Being* — has been cited as a major contribution to the field. Extensive presentations and panel discussions focused on the use of music therapy. Special attention was focused upon the needs of the elderly at this conference.

The late Dr. Howard A. Rusk cited the conference and the proceedings books that emerged from the conference as an important contribution to a neglected area of medical care. He stated: "To rehabilitation medicine it adds a new and vibrant dimension; and to patients, a holistic approach to care." (Rusk, 1989) (See Appendix 5.)

The third conference which was hosted by Dr. Lee in 1990 — *Current Research in Music Therapy* — focused on the state of the art of research in music therapy. Again, special presentations were focused on the needs of the elderly and the current state of treatment and research in music therapy.

Currently, Dr. Lee serves as senior vice president of MedArt USA, a non-profit organization founded to "bring the arts to medicine and medicine to the arts" (see Appendix 4,C), and is preparing for *MedArt International's First World Congress on Arts and Medicine*, to be held in New York City February 26-March 1, 1992. At this congress, many of the courses, workshops and free papers specifically report on the use of music therapy and the elderly.

As an author and an editor, Dr. Lee has written extensively on the subjects of rehabilitation, geriatric medical care, functionality, music therapy, technology and chronic pain. His extensive bibliography displays a broad range of insight and expertise on many of today's most pressing health needs for the elderly.

C.   CLINICAL EXPERIENCE AND FUTURE GOALS

By integrating music and music therapy with the environment of the elderly, many limitations on functional independence may well be removed. Specifically, through the intervention of music therapy, reduced use of medications without consequent diminished function may well result, thereby enhancing safety, attention, mobility and independence. Clearly, music therapy in its various forms can facilitate cost containment and cost effectiveness in the health care of the elderly at home or in institutionsl. Some of the specific areas of application are described as follows:

1.   Falls

Extensive clinical case studies show the intricate nature of the causes of falls in the elderly. Literature mentions loss of balance, loss or proprioception, weakness in the ankle muscles, peripheral nerve damage, multiple drug intake, decreased attention span, and many other causes. Often, the causes are multiple. Music addresses in essence all or most of these causes, either through rhythmic cues, or through increased proprioception, or through enhanced attention span. Remarkable gains were made in many patients presenting with gait disturbances due to one or more of these causes with the use of music and audiovisual biofeedback.

Falls leading very commonly to hip fractures, and hip fractures being the 'beginning of the end' for most elderly, including lengthy stays in nursing homes, if it can at all contribute to decreasing their incidence, music would certainly demonstrate its cost effectiveness in health care. The price to pay would be minimal. The ultimate goal is always to keep these patients functioning as independently as possible and out of any health care institution.

2. **Assistive Technology**

A great number of older adults, with minor or major disabilities, must rely on a large panoply of assistive devices, ranging from the common cane to the most sophisticated electronic wheelchair. Clinical experience shows that this technology is more-or-less well-received, its functioning more-or-less well-understood in this population. Often times, it is put in the closet after brief use, for many reasons: breakdown, complexity of use, depressing appearance, lack of interaction, etc. One notices very often in this population a tendency to a negative outlook on life, coupled with self-ageism and decreased life satisfaction. All of these behavioral and emotional trends directly interfere with any treatment, let alone the use of mechanical or electronic devices. It has been our experience that devices that are interactive in nature, especially those using audiovisual feedback, are more likely to be used and therefore fulfill their purpose. Assistive devices are extremely costly to the health care system. Maximizing their use and minimizing their redundant prescription is more than likely to achieve their cost effectiveness.

3. **Pain Management**

Chronic pain, especially of a musculoskeletal nature such as low back pain, arthritis and osteoporosis, is one of the primary epidemics of our modern era. One of the most difficult problems in dealing with patients with chronic intractable pain, prevalent among the elderly, was the paucity of objective measurement tools. Indeed, the subjective component is often overwhelming and very difficult to assess. Modern technology such as the simple-to-use and non-invasive thermography techniques now allow us to measure the direct effect of any therapy on pain (Appendix 3,A). The use of these tools is more and more widespread in clinical practice. The Rusk Institute pioneered in the use of thermography for assessment of pain, especially after music therapy and continues to serve in a leadership role in this important programmatic research effort.

4. **Chronic Neurological Conditions**

This encompasses a great number of rehabilitation patients. Diagnoses such as stroke, multiple sclerosis, and Parkinson's disease are very common in a rehabilitation medicine unit. Here again, music and recreation therapy have been found to be excellent adjuncts to the more conventional occupational and physical therapies. These patients often are afflicted with several deficits: speech, upper- and lower extremity motion, attention span, etc. Musical interventions have been found to facilitate the therapeutic process in all or most of these deficits. For example, often times, a stroke patient with upper-extremity deficit an d slight aphasia has been motivated by music to clap his/her hands and sing along in a music therapy session, thus enhancing and speeding the recovery process (Appendix 6).

5. **Respiratory Diseases**

Acute or chronic, these diseases are often fatal in the elderly population. Many bedridden hospitalized patients afflicted with one or more of the above conditions can suffer intercurrent respiratory problems such as pneumonia or bronchitis during their hospital stay. Very often, these respiratory diseases are triggered by ill-breathing and stagnation of secretions. Clinical experience has shown the very beneficial effect of singing and the use of musical instruments to enhance breathing and expectoration in this population. Clinical studies are now under way to help demonstrate this. Often, an intercurrent acute respiratory ailment means forced bed confinement for a stroke patient, away from the daily therapy, thus leading to a number of other severe complications such as bedsores, urinary tract infections, thrombophlebitis and pulmonary emboli. This vicious cycle is often fatal for the patient, not to mention the exponential rise in health care costs. Wouldn't it be great is simple daily singing could help prevent such an unfortunate course?

In his keynote address during the *Fourth International Symposium on Music, Rehabilitation and Human Well-Being* (Appendix 4,A) — which was to be his last public appearance — Senator Jacob Javits, then a patient at the Rusk Institute, said: "This is a unique therapy and is a great boon to the disabled, as it should be, as it must be, seriously undertaken as an element of medicine. . ." (Appendix 6).

D. **RECOMMENDED RESEARCH**

Although anecdotal clinical experience and a limited number of research studies with the elderly all confirm the benefits of music therapy in preventing potentially fatal conditions, enhancing patients' well-being, shortening their hospital stay and increasing their independence thereafter, many longitudinal double-blind controlled studies are now necessary to produce scientific evidence on the effectiveness of music therapy in the health care delivery system. This task is nowadays greatly enhanced by the availability of objective measurement tools, as previously outlined in this text.

It is our opinion that a significant effort should be made at the level of the federal government to encourage research in this area. As America becomes greyer, this research will affect an ever-growing number of its citizens. In these days of economic hardship and escalating health care costs, the search for alternative non-invasive and less costly therapies should be a necessary focus of legislators.

RFPs based on the priority area of "therapeutic effects of music and the creative arts therapies" are long overdue. Sufficient evidence has been gathered through pilot- and case studies to warrant such a step. More than 100 music therapists nationwide have obtained a Ph.D. degree and are fully trained in scholarly and academic research, and should be encouraged to pursue a career in this field. Upon publication of the first such RFP in the Federal Register, no doubt a large number of competitive research grant proposals will be submitted, thus corroborating the above. For example, the following could be used as models:

- **Demonstration projects** expand music therapy services to facilities offering services to older adults, their families and their communities. For example, innovative programs for persons diagnosed with Alzheimer's disease and their caregivers can evaluate new techniques in the community.

- **Basic research** may document specific processes involving the influence of music on behavior. For example, research on the neurological and physical effects of music involve the use of state-of-the-art technology.

- **Clinical outcome research** provides much needed evaluation of treatment effects. For example, research on the effect of music therapy on patients' length of hospital stay or need for medication has implications for health care costs, e.g. Medicare.

Planning should be undertaken towards the establishment of a Center for Music in Medicine, as part of the National Institute on Aging or the National Institute of Child Health and Development, with its own separate funding appropriation. The staff of the Rusk Institute would be honored to serve as part of the planning committee.

E.   CONCLUSIONS

In our society, the elderly are often viewed as declining in function and ability and as having limited potential to learn, improve and develop new skills. Such attitudes serve to set minimal levels of aspiration for our elderly population and the overwhelming evidence clearly indicates that this view is wrong, unfair and contrary to the facts. Music and music therapy enhance the functional capabilities of the elderly as well as raise their level of aspiration and potential to more realistic levels. They can learn, function, enjoy and maintain an independent quality of life if given the tools, environment, support and resources.

BIBLIOGRAPHY

AARP: Understanding senior housing for the 1990's an American Association of Retired Persons survey of consumer preferences, concerns and need, 10, 1990.

Ashley MG, Gryfe CE, Amies A: A longitudinal study of falls in an elderly population. II. Some circumstances of falling. *Age Ageing* 1977; 6:211-220.

Aspen Institutes Forum Report #2, 1987.

Bailey LM: Music's soothin charms. *Pain Consult* 1985;(11) 1280-1281.

Baker SP, Harvey AH: Fall Injuries in the Elderly. *Clinics in Geriatric Med* 1985; 1(3):501-512.

Bennett SL, Maas F: The effect of music-based life review on the life satisfaction and ego integrity of elderly people. *Brit J Occ Ther* 1988;51(12):433-436.

Blair SN, Jacobs DR, Powell KE: Relationships between exercise or physical activity and other health behaviors. *Public Health Rep* 1985;109:172-80.

Bonny HL: Music and Healing. *Music Ther* 1986; 6A(1):3-12.

Bonny LH: Music listening for intensive coronary care units: A pilot project. *Music Ther* 1983;3(1):4-16.

Borden P, Vanderheiden G, Berliss J, Esser S, Devine A, and Dega S: Dissemination of information on communication, control, and computer access. Trace Research and Development Center, University of Wisconsin, 1989.

Botte MJ, Waters RL, Keenan MA, Jordan C, Garland DE: Orthopaedic management of the stroke patient, Part 2: Treatment deformities of the upper and   lower extremities. *Orthopaedic Rev* 1988; 17(9):891-909.

Botte MJ, Waters RL, Keenan MA, Jordan C, Garland DE: Orthopaedic management of the stroke patient, Part 1: Pathophysiology, limb deformity and patient evaluation. *Orthopaedic Rev* 1988; 17(6):637-646.

Bright R: Music in Geriatric Care. New York, St. Martin's press, 1972.

Brocklehurst JC, Robertson D, James-Groom P. Clinical correlates of sway in old age-sensory modalities. *Age Ageing* 1982; 11:1-10.

Campbell AJ, Reinken J, Allan BC, Martinez GS: Falls in old age: A study of frequency and related clinical factors. *Age Ageing* 1981; 10:264-270.

Caspersen CJ, Christenson GM, Pollard RA: Status of the 1990 physical fitness and exercise objectives-evidence from NHIS 1985. *Public Health Rep* 1986;101:587-92.

CDC: Surgeon General's Workshop on Health Promotion and Aging: Summary Recommendations of Physical Fitness and Exercise Working Group. *JAMA* 1989;262(18)2507-2510

Cook JA: Music as an intervention in the oncology setting. *Career Nursing* 1986;8(1):23-28.

Cooper C, Barker DJP, Wickham C: Physical activity, muscle strength, and calcium intake in fracture of proximal femur in Britian *Br Med J* 1988;297:1443-6.

Davie JW, Blumenthal MD, Robinson-Hawkins S: A model of risk of falling for psychogeriatric patients. *Arch. Gen. Psychiatry* 1981; 38:463-467.

Davis-Rollans C, Cuningham SG: Physiologic responses of coronary care patients to selected music. *Heart & Lung* 1987;16(4)370-378.

deVries HA: Prescription of exercise for older men from telemented exercise heart rate data. *Geriatrics* 1971;26:102.

Elkowitz EB, Elkowitz D: Adding life to later years through exercise. *Postgraduate Medicine* 1986;80(3):91-103.

Fernie GR, Gryfe CI, Holliday PJ, Llewellyn A: The relationship of postural sway in standing to the incidence of falls in geriatric subjects. *Age Ageing* 1982; 11:11-16.

Gilbert JP: Music therapy perspectives on death and dying. *J Music Ther* 1977;14(4):165-171.

Glynn NJ: The therapy of Music. *J Gerontological Nursing* 1986; 12(1):6-10.

Gorman KM, Posner JD: Benefits of exercise in Old Age. *Clinics in Geriatric Medicine* 1988; 4(1):181-192.

Greenfield DG: The evaluation of a computer system for behavioral observation   training and research. *J Music Ther* 1985; 22:95-98.

Gregory D, Sims W: Music preference analysis with computers *J Music Ther* 1987; 24(4):203-212.

Gryfe CI, Ameiss A, Ashley MJ: A longitudinal study of falls in an elderly population: Incidence and morbidity. *Age Ageing* 1977; 6:201-210.

Guimaraes RM, Isaacs B: Characteristics of the gait of old people who fall. *Int Rehabil Med* 1980; 2:177-180.

Hamdy R, Zakaria G: A special clinic for the over-65's in a G.P. surgery. *Practitioner* 1977; 219:365-375.

Hoyt DR, Creech JC: The life satisfaction index: A methodological and theoretical critique. *J of Gerontology* 1983; 38(1):111-116.

Hurwitz L: Neurological aspects of old age and capacity. *Gerontol Clin* 1968; 10:146-156.

Imms FJ, Edholm OG: Studies of gait and mobility in the elderly. *Age Ageing* 1981; 10:147-156.

Kemp B, Brummel-Smith K, Ramsdell JW: Geriatric Rehabilitation. *Little, Brown and Company* 1990.

Kirshen A, Cape RDT, Hayes HC, Spencer JD: Postural sway and cardiovascular parameters associated with falls in elderly. *J Clin Esp Geron* 1984; 6:291-307.

Knapp RB, Lusted HS: A bioelectric controller for computer music applications. *Computer Music J* 1990; 14(1):42-47.

Kokmen E, Bossemeyer RW, Williams W: Quantitative evaluation of joint motion sensation in an aging population. *J. Gerontol* 1987; 33:62-67.

Koller WC, Glatt SL, Fox JH: Senile Gait, A distinct neurologic entity. *Clinics in Geriatric Med* 1985; 1(3):661-669.

Krout RE: MusicShapes. *Research in Developmental Disabilities* 1988; 9:105-108.

Krout, RE: *Microcomputer applications in music therapy* 1988; Columbia University Teacher's College, New York, NY.

Krout RE: Evaluating software for music therapy applications. *J Music Ther* 1987; 24(4):213-223.

Krout RE, Mason M: Information Sharing: Using computer and electronic music resources in clinical music therapy with behavior disordered students, 12 to 18 years old. *Music Ther Perspectives* 1988; 5:114-118.

Krout, RE: Information Sharing: The microcomputing music therapist. *J Ther Perspectives* 1987; 4:64-67.

Lane JM, Healey JH, Bansal M, Levine B: Overview of geriatric osteopenic syndromes; Part I: Definition and pathophysiology. *Orthop Review* 1988; 17(11):1131-1139.

Larsson L, Grimby G, Karlsson F: Muscle strength and speed of movement in relation to age and muscle morphology. *J Appl Physiol* 1979; 46:451-456.

Lichtenstein MJ, Sheilds SL, Shiavi RG, Burger MC: Exercise and balance in aged women: A pilot controlled clinical trial. *Arch Phys Med Rehabil* 1989; 70(2):138-143.

MacDonald JB: The role of drugs in falls in the elderly: *Clinics in Geriatr. Med.* 1985; 1(3):621-631.

Melcher J, Fisk CF, Heinz J, Azvedo I: *Aging America-Trends and Projections.* 1987-1988 edition.

Melton LJ, Riggs BL: Risk factors for injury after a fall. *Clinics in Geriatric Medicine* 1985; 1(3):525-539.

Millar AP: Realistic exercise goals for the elderly: is feeling good enough? *Geriatrics* 1987; 42(3):25-29.

Milligan E: Will you join the dance. *Physiotherapy* 1986; 72(9):475-478.

Monahan JA: The changing face of geriatrics. *The New York Doctor* 1988; 1(16):1-3.

Mossey JM: Social and psychologic factors related to falls among the elderly. *Clinics in Geriatric Med* 1985; 1(3):541-553.

Munoz E, Johnson H, Margolis I, Ratner L, Mulloy K, Wise L: DRG's orthopedic surgery, and age at an academic medical center. *DRG Reimbursement System* 1988; 11(12):1645-1651.

Nagler JC: Technology and music therapy. *Closing the Gap* 1986; 5(2);13 and 18.

Nagler JC, Lee MHM: Music therapy using computer music technology. In MHM Lee (Ed.), *Rehabilitation, music and human well-being* 1989; St. Louis, Missouri, MMB Music: 226-241.

Nagler JC, Lee MHM: Use of microcomputers in the music therapy process of a post viral encephalitic musician. *Med Problems of Performing Artists* 1987; 2(2):72-74.

Nagler JC: The Biomuse. *Active Sensing* 1989; 1(3):13 and 15.

NIH Report of the Task Force on Medical Rehabilitation Research. Information Resources. Hunt Valley, MD 1990.

Nordoff P, Robbins C: *Creative music Ther* 1977; New York, NY: The John Day Company.

Nordoff P, Robbins C: *Music ther special educ* (2nd ed.) 1983; St. Louis,MO: MMB Music.

Obara, KE: *Computers in music ther: A survey of computer uses by music therapists.* Unpublished manuscript, Little City Foundation, Palatine,Illinois; 1985.

Ochs AL, Newberry J, Leinhardt ML, Harkins SW: Neural and vestibular aging associated with falls. In Birreny, J., Schaie, K.W. (eds.): Handbook of psychology of aging. New York: Van Nostrand Reinhold Co., 1985, 378-399.

Overstall PW, Johnson AL, Exton-Smith AN: Instability and falls in the elderly. *Age Ageing* 1978; 7:92s-96s.

Overstall PW, Exton-Smith AN, Imms FJ, Johnson AL: Falls in elderly related to postural imbalance. *Br Med J* 1977; 1:261-264.

Overstall PW, Exton-Smith AN, Imms FJ, Johnson AL: Falls in the elderly related to postural imbalance. *Br Med J* 1977; 1:261-264.

Pfaffenberger RS, Wing AL, Hyde RT, Jung DL: Physical activity and incidence of hypertension in college alumni. *Am J Epidemiol* 1983;117:245-57.

Palmer MD: Music therapy in a comprehensive program of treatment and rehabilitation for the geriatric resident. *J Music Ther* 1977; 14(4):190-197.

Perret E, Regli F: Age and perceptual threshold for vibratory stimuli. Eur Neurol. 1970; 4:65-76.

Perry BC: Falls among elderly living in high-rise apartments. *J Fam Pract* 1982; 14:1069-1073.

Phillips JR: Music in the nursing of elderly persons in nursing homes. *J Gerontological Nursing* 1980; 6(1):37-39.

Pokras R: Diagnosis-related groups using data from the National Hospital Discharge Survey: United States, 1981. NCHS Advance data no. 98, U.S. Department of Health and Human Services, Washington, D.C., 1984.

Potman R: A speech controlled environmental control. Sponsor: Innovative Research Programme/Aide for Handicapped, Enshede, The Netherlands, 1980.

Potvin AR, Syndulko K, Tourtellotte WW, et al.: Human neurologic function and the aging process. *J Am Geriatr Soc* 1980; 28:1-9.

Powell KE, Thompson PD, Caspersen CJ, Kendrick JS: Physical activity and the incidence of coronary heart disease. *Ann Rev Public Health* 1987;8:253-87.

Prosper V: Design features, housing older New Yorkers. NY State Department of Housing Report, 1990; 1.

Prudham D, Evans, JG: Factors associated with falls in the elderly: A community study. *Age Ageing* 1981; 10:141-146.

Rabinowitz M: La marche:une importance cognitive et sensorielle fondamentale. *Actualities en Gerontologie* 1982; 8:(30)15-20.

Salmon P, Newmark J: Clinical applications of MIDI technology. *Medical Problems of Performing Artists* 1990; 5(1):25-31.

Simpson WM: Exercise: Prescriptions for the Elderly. *Geriatrics* 1986;41(1):95-100.

Skinner HB, Barrack RL, Cook SD: Age-related decline in proprioception. *Clin Orthop* 1984; 184:208-211.

Smith GH: A comparison of the effects of three treatment interventions on cognitive functioning of Alzheimer patients. *Music Ther* 1986; 61(1):41-56.

Smith EL, Gilligan C: Physical Activity Prescription for the Older Adult. *Phy and Sports Med* 1983;11(8):91-101.

Spirduso WW: Physical fitness, aging, and psychomotor speed: A review. *J Gerontol* 1980; 35(6):850.

Spirduso WW: Reaction and movement time as a function of age and physical activity level. *J Gerontol* 1975; 33:435.

Spitzer S: Computers and music therapy: An integrated approach. Four case studies. *Music Ther Perspectives* 1989; (6):51-54.

Staum MJ: Music and rhythmic stimuli in the rehabilitation of gait disorders. *J Music Ther* 1983; 20(2):69-87.

Steiness I: Vibratory perception in normal subjects. *Acta Med Scand* 1957; 158:315-325.

Stoedefalke KG: Motivating and substaining the older adult in an exercise program. *TGR* 1985;1(1), 78-83.

Task Force on Prescription Drugs, U.S. Dept. of H.E.W.: The Drug Users. Washington, D.C., Government Printing Office, 1968.

Tideiksaar R: Environment adaptations to preserve balance and prevent falls. *Top Geriatr Rehabil* 1990;5(2):78-84.

Tinetti ME: Performance-oriented assessment of mobility problems in elderly patients. *J Am Geriatr Soc* 1986; 34:119-126.

Titiloye VM: The Relationship of age to premotor reaction time, motor reaction time and movement time performance of a functional activity in adult females. Unpublished Doctoral Thesis, New York University, 1988.

Tobas TS, Mayak L, Hoehler F: Visual perception of verticality and horizontality among elderly fallers. *Arch Phys Med Rehab* 1981; 62:619-622.

Tomaino CM: Music therapy in reality orientation with institutionalized elderly with dementia. Unpublished Master's Thesis, New York University, 1979.

Trimble J, Nemchausky B, Ozer M, Hooker E, Johnson P, Kafka R, Seal E: Interactive videodisk training for self-care skills. *Rehabilitation R&D Center*, Edward Hines Jr. VA Hospital, Hines, Illinois, 1989.

Vanderark S, Newman I, Bell S: The effects of music participation on quality of life of the elderly. *Music Ther* 1983; 3(1):71-81.

Vanderheiden G, Schauer J, Kelso D: Interconnection standards for electrical and electronic devices (InterSEED) for people with disabilities. *Trace Research and Development Center*, 1989, Waisman Center on Mental Retardation and Human Development, University of Wisconsin, Madison, Madison, Wisconsin.

Vanderheiden G, Lee C, Velso D: Considerations in the design of computers and operating systems to increase their accessibility to persons with disabilities.Trace Research and Development Center, Madison Wisconson, 1989.

Wild D, Nayak USL, Isaacs B: How dangerous are falls in old people at home? *Br Med J* 1981; 282:266-268.

Wild D, Nayak USL, Isaacs B: Prognosis of falls in old people at home. *J Epidemiol Community Health* 1981; 35:200-204.

Williamson J: Prescribing problems in the elderly. *Practitioner* 1978; 220:749-755.

Wolfe JR: The use of music in a group sensory training program for regressed geriatric patients. *Activities, Adaptation & Aging* 1983; 4(1);49-61.

Wolfson LI, Whipple R, Amerman P, Kaplan J, Kleinberg A: Gait and balance in the elderly; Two functional capacities that link sensory and motor ability to falls. *Clinics in Geriatr Med* 1985; 1(3):649-659.

APPENDICES

Senator REID. Thank you very much, Dr. Lee.
We'll hear now from our last witness, Dr. Frank Wilson.
Doctor Wilson.

STATEMENT OF FRANK WILSON, M.D., DANVILLE, CA

Dr. WILSON. Thank you, Senator Reid and Senator Cohen.

I wish to also thank you for the opportunity to participate in today's hearing, which I think has probably already proven to be a landmark occasion in the history of this Committee. I am honored to do what I can to advance the result.

To begin, I would like to share with you several conclusions drawn from more than a decade of involvement in the issue that you are addressing here today.

All humans are innately musical. By this I mean we are biologically endowed with the ability to create and respond to music. This aptitude is as deeply routed in the nervous system and as integral to life as is the gift of language.

Neither age nor physical disadvantage is a bar to active participation in music or to sharing in its diverse and substantial benefits.

Musical achievement—what we do with our musical birthright—has far more to do with training and experience than with what is called "talent." The process can be started at any age, and requires little more than an eager student and a sympathetic, skillful teacher. It is never too late to learn.

Music has great potential in both medical and rehabilitation treatment protocols. It is largely ignored as a subject for medical research, and it is significantly under-utilized in medical practice.

As a neurologist, I am intrigued at the multiplicity of musical forms and its remarkable influence on human development and maturation. I suspect that something like the following is true—music arises spontaneously from a brain whose operations are inherently rhythmic, harmonic, patterned, and sequential. Perhaps this is why it is both a stimulus and a powerful organizer of movement, thought, language, emotion, personal action, and social interaction, and why it retains this power throughout life.

If I may, I would like now to describe briefly the path that led me to these conclusions.

I am a neurologist, and I began full-time practice with the Permanente Medical Group of Northern California 23 years ago. My own development as a physician has been deeply influenced by many colleagues and a professional situation emphasizing high-quality health care that is both humanitarian and economical. It is fundamental to our philosophy that a patient become an informed, active partner through education, and the fostering of personal attitudes and strategies which promote health and well-being. To me, education for life and education for health mean the same thing.

It was not obvious to me until just a few years ago that adding education for music would give us a third component in this strategy for a fuller and healthier life. I owe it to my own piano teacher, Lillian Bauer Cox, that I discovered I didn't have to spend the rest of my life standing outside the window looking in at the musicians.

Lillian, who was my daughter's piano teacher, had asked me to give a talk on the brain to her students. "They'd love to know how the brain makes the fingers go" is how she put it. I gave the talk, and Lillian rewarded me with three free piano lessons. "Who knows?" she said, "You might enjoy it." She was right. For 5 years I studied piano with her, having so much fun I could not understand why more people my age didn't study music. I decided the answer had more to do with the way people were taught than with any innate incapacity to learn.

So I decided to write a book about my experience. The book, called "Tone Deaf and All Thumbs," was intended to refute the widely held belief that music belongs to specially gifted people who demonstrate their precocity at the age of 3 and are put on the Juilliard admission list when they are 5 or 6. The book brought me quite a few interesting letters from other adult beginners, most of whom said they owed their success to a teacher who didn't know the meaning of the term nonmusician.

The research I did for the book had another consequence. I became interested in finding other health professionals, scientists, and educators who might have something to say about the physical side of music making. In 1983, I met Professor Franz Roehmann at the University of Colorado in Denver, who is here with us today. He offered to help organize a conference in Denver called "The Biology of Music Making," which was held in 1984. This was so successful that we decided to do a second, "Music and Child Development," held again in Denver in the summer of 1987. And just 2 weeks ago we held our third conference—"Music, Growth, and Aging"—at the University of Rochester. We have published books based on the two conferences I described, and are now working on the manuscript for the third.

One of the important outcomes of the Biology of Music Making Conferences has been the clarification of an agenda for building on what has already been learned. I am submitting to you today, as an example of such a proposal, a proposal for a Music Development Research Institute, which we prepared last year as part of a long-range development plan involving a number of interested institutions.

In conclusion, I would like to tell you about my hopes for the future. We have much to learn about music in human life. We need better ways to bring artists, scientists, medical practitioners, and educators together more effectively.

I cannot say enough to praise the commitment to interdisciplinary research and education which exists at the University of Rochester, where the Eastman School of Music and the School of Medicine and Dentistry have formally established programs to sponsor new work and to foster new careers linking music with biologic, behavior, and medical science, and where studies on aging and health already represent a high research priority. Similar efforts are being discussed and planned at the University of Colorado in Denver, the University of California in San Francisco, and other universities. But these remain fledgling programs, and they deserve far greater recognition and support than is presently available.

What you are doing here today could be an important first step in creating a national initiative for musical opportunity for our entire population.

Thank you.

[The prepared statement of Dr. Wilson follows:]

Special Committee on Aging
United States Senate

August 1, 1991

Statement of Frank R. Wilson, M.D.

Neurologist, Permanente Medical Group, Northern California

Associate Clinical Professor of Neurology
University of California, San Francisco

Founder and Vice-President
The Biology of Music Making, Inc.

The Musical Development Research Institute

I. The Proposal

The Biology of Music Making, Inc., in cooperation with university affiliates, and anticipating the emergence of a new scientific discipline, will establish the Musical Development Research Institute. Its mission will be to:

- Carry out basic research in biomechanical, motor and perceptual correlates of musical performance
- Offer research and technical training to industrial and design engineers, clinicians, music educators and other professionals and graduate students in preparation for career work in performing arts medicine, musical instrument ergonomics, and basic research in human musical skills
- Publish research, conduct symposia and workshops, and engage in public information activities
- Consult with private industry and with clinical entities concerning health problems of musicians and others whose work involves skilled use of the hands
- Recruit a staff of research professionals and consultants, emphasizing the collaboration of bioengineers, neurobiologists, psychophysicists and movement and behavioral scientists
- Create a self-supporting, state-of-the-art research facility

II. Organizational background

The Biology of Music Making, Inc. is a nonprofit, tax exempt educational organization incorporated in Colorado in 1984. The Board of Directors consists of:

President Franz L. Roehmann, Ph.D., Professor of Music, University of Colorado, Denver
Vice President Frank R. Wilson, M.D., Associate Clinical Professor of Neurology, and Director of Education/Research, Health Program for Performing Artists, University of California, San Francisco
Secretary-Treasurer Patricia L. Wilson

Consultants to the Biology of Music Making are:

Physiology George Moore, Ph.D., formerly Professor of Biomedical Engineering, University of Southern California
Biomechanics Dr. med. Christoph Wagner, Professor of Physiology of Music, Hochschule für Musik und Theater, Hannover, Germany
Computers Bob L. Berschauer, President, MicroBusiness Instruction
Publications Norman Goldberg, President, MMB Music, Inc., St. Louis

The Biology of Music Making has conducted two international conferences at the University of Colorado, and held its third conference at the University of Rochester in July, 1991. Proceedings from the first two conferences (*The Biology of Music Making, 1987; Music and Child Development, 1990*) are published. Total grants in excess of $150,000 have been received for conference and publishing projects to date; major contributors include:

- National Association of Music Merchants
- Yamaha Music Corporation, USA
- IBM Fund for Community Services
- Apple Computers
- Baldwin Piano & Organ Company
- Kaiser Family Foundation
- University of Colorado, Denver
- Denver Center for the Performing Arts

III. Proposal background

Through our conferences and through resulting contacts with clinicians, scientists and educators in the United States and abroad, we have become increasingly aware of the limitations faced by those attempting to conduct basic research into the biological basis of musical performance. Such efforts are hampered not only by financial restrictions but by deficiencies in the scientific skills and protocols demanded for meaningful research.

Movement—or *motor skills*—science, for example, is a comparatively new but complex and demanding discipline currently pursued in only a few laboratories in the world, where few musicians have visited or worked. Moreover, almost none of the people working in these laboratories is familiar with the particulars of musical training.

During the 1989-1990 academic year, Dr. Wilson served as Guest Professor of Neurology at the University of Düsseldorf in West Germany. His research there involved the study of a severe occupational disorder of musicians called focal dystonia. Work was carried out using pianos, a computer and software donated by Yamaha Europa and Yamaha Music Corporation, USA.

Professors Wagner and Moore, both consultants to The Biology of Music Making, participated in this project, and the findings of the study have been presented at two national conferences (American Academy of Neurology and American College of Occupational Medicine conferences in 1991). A major conclusion is that this disorder stems from the interaction of individual physical characteristics, inappropriate training, and mechanical characteristics of the instruments being played. The implications for music pedagogy and instrument design, manufacture and marketing are substantial.

So far as we know, opportunities for research of this kind are rare, and will remain so until a way is found to create an environment where the full potential of research into the physical basis of musical skill can be exploited. It is that goal to which the Directors of the Biology of Music Making, Inc. are now committed.

IV. Prospects for strengthening the arts-medicine liaison

The Biology of Music Making, Inc. has been an active participant and an influential voice within the growing arts-medicine community. The past decade has seen the formation of special clinics for performing artists within major urban medical centers (New York, Philadelphia, Boston, Chicago, Cleveland, Houston and San Francisco being the most prominent).

The Institute will be a primary source of information and training for those interested in developing research skills. Specifically, individuals undergoing training at the Institute will be qualified to work toward:

- Improved understanding of the physiological and biomechanical factors influencing individual performance
- Improved understanding of optimal training protocols for development of musical proficiency for all individuals, including the elderly and the disabled
- Improved understanding of the musician-instrument interface; optimizing instrumental design with respect to acoustic and biomechanical parameters and individual physical variability
- Improved objectivity in diagnosis of performance related problems
- Improved treatment of performance related injuries; where possible, basing therapies on scientifically validated ergonomic and training principles

V. Rationale for additional support:

In the seven years of its existence, the Biology of Music Making has established itself as an innovative and powerful catalyst for interdisciplinary research and education involving several medical communities, and professionals in music performance and education. Our ability to carry out this work has depended on computer technology for data management, communications and publications. As we expand our efforts, our agenda and our contacts, we will increasingly be involved in education and research design and training at the University level.

There can be no question that Institute work will generate heightened interest in MIDI (Musical Instrument Digital Interface) technology as a basic research tool in music performance research, and could easily stimulate commercially important new technology for the study of *all* human skilled performance.

The Institute would become an authoritative source of information about optimal design of musical instruments, and the adaptation of computer and synthesizer technology to individual training requirements and goals. By improving access to instruments and linking pedagogic strategies to scientific studies of movement, the Institute could make a major contribution to the popularization of music instrument study.

VI. Endowment goal: $5 million

The exact costs of establishment of the Institute can only be roughly estimated. The endowment estimate of $5 million contemplates special building design and scientific instrumentation, full-time administrative, technical and research staff, communication, computer, conference, publication and library facilities and support for consultant activities. It is known that the costs for establishing the well known acoustic and voice research facilities in Paris, Stockholm and Denver, were equal to or considerably in excess of this amount.

VII. Summary

No single profession, industry segment or academic institution has the immediate potential for embracing or pursuing Institute goals independently. Encouraged as we may be by the success of our efforts and activities to date, we are nevertheless sobered by the magnitude of the effort that would be required to advance to a higher level of commitment or involvement. Not only has no other organization managed to develop an institute of the kind we propose, no one has even attempted to do so. The proposed Musical Development Research Institute represents an entirely unique conceptual solution to the most crucial challenges facing music performance medicine and research.

The Biology of Music Making, Inc.

(Revised August 1, 1991)

Franz L. Roehmann, President

Frank R. Wilson, Vice-President

Senator REID. Thank you, Dr. Wilson.

Before I ask questions I want to just mention and extend my appreciation for Senator Cohen for participating so thoroughly in today's hearing. For those of you in the audience who don't know—and many of you do—Senator Cohen has a particular interest in the arts. He is a part-time Senator and a full-time author. He truly spends the same time we all do being a Senator, but any spare time he has he is an author. He has a book that is fascinating called "One-Eyed Kings," which I read as a gesture of friendship toward him, and then after I got through the first 3 or 4 pages I did it because that's what I wanted to do. It was exciting. He is a poet. And so anything dealing with the arts is something he has particular interest in.

Bill, I appreciate very much your being here today and allowing us to use your expertise.

We are going to work together to try to do some of the things that this hearing has brought to our minds.

Dr. Clair, I appreciate very much your outlining some of the studies that we could conduct that would be beneficial. You outline those in some detail, and it gives us pinpointed subjects that I'm sure we can spend a few dollars on that would save this Government, in effect, with Medicare and other programs, a hundredfold of what we would spend on those small programs. I appreciate that direction.

All of your written statements will be made a part of the record in their entirety.

Your testimony outlines specifically what we, as a Congress, need to do to project out some of this music therapy making people well. Thank you very much for your diligence in that regard.

Dr. Lee, do you really think music therapy can save on Federal expenditures? If so, why do you say that?

Dr. LEE. The answer is yes. I will give you an example.

If one looks at the amount of medication that is given in nursing homes, primarily they would fall into two categories—one, to help a patient sleep; the other, to reduce pain.

It is my contention and my clinical observations up to this point in time that if we play music or any form of creative art, we'll reduce the amount of medication that is given.

What I would like to do, then, is to translate this money that is saved from the pharmacy department and use it to hire a music therapist.

Senator REID. Dr. Lee, is it fair to say, then, that music therapy is totally underutilized—if, in fact, it is utilized at all—by doctors, hospitals, and extended care facilities? Is that true?

Dr. LEE. Yes. And I think that this hearing will add light to this dimension. I have told music therapists many times that to break into the medical center or hospital circle is awfully difficult, particularly in our budget crisis now. They are going to say, "Why should I hire a music therapist when I need a nurse?" They don't look at cost containment, unfortunately.

Senator REID. And that's one of the primary reasons, of course to employ music therapy. By not doing so, we are penny wise and pound foolish.

Dr. LEE. Yes, sir.

Senator REID. Dr. Clair, what you see is so much more meaningful than what someone tells you, and we saw what you can do on video today. It is magic. Is there any other way to describe what you are able to do with music?

Dr. CLAIR. Actually, I think through very careful observation and trying to notice the very slight responses, we have been able to tap residual skills and abilities that were not evident before. And through our research with looking at what kinds of things elderly persons can do—particularly those who are demented—we have been able to build on that knowledge base. So I'm not sure it is just magic.

Senator REID. As a music therapist with the extensive experience that you have, would you tell us in your own words some of the ways that music therapy improves the lives of older Americans?

Dr. CLAIR. It probably provides quality of life by giving opportunities for successful experience, for social interaction, for some of those opportunities that have been lost through physical restrictions, through various other kinds of disabilities, and also through the types of contacts that older people lose, even if they are well. For instance, their friends die. They may have to relocate. They may often move to the town where their children live. There are all kinds of reasons why they lose the social contact.

We have already heard from physicians about the physiological responses that happen, and a lot of those we don't clearly understand yet.

So I think probably the social, the physical, and the emotional opportunities to express, to share, to interact with others, to have feelings of belonging, and to just basically have opportunities for self-expression that may not otherwise be there.

Senator REID. One last question. Are there schools that give degrees in music therapy?

Dr. CLAIR. Yes.

Senator REID. Tell me about them. Are there many?

Dr. CLAIR. I believe there are over 65. The University of Kansas had the first degree program for music therapy in 1946, so it has been there for a very long time. These schools are spread throughout the country. Some of them offer the basic bachelor's degree. But there are several that offer the master's degree, and several that offer the doctoral program, Ph.D.

Senator REID. Senator Cohen.

Senator COHEN. Mr. Chairman, I have been sitting here thinking how I can respond in a modest way to an overly generous statement made by the Chairman. I think that there are probably three ways. There is the Harvard way, the Yale way, and the Maine way. The Harvard way was typified by A. Lawrence Lowell, who said that flattery is like nicotine—not harmful unless deeply inhaled. The Yale way was expressed by Robert Maynard Hutchins, who said, upon being introduced one time, "That was the most thoroughly researched, the most eloquently delivered, and the most richly deserved introduction that I have ever had." The Maine way would simply say, "Thank you for your generosity. Far more generous than just."

Music, in a way, is very much like poetry. They are inter-related. Robert Frost said that every poem is a stay against the confusion of the world. I think that is particularly true of music, as well. It is a stay against that confusion and the disorder and the sometimes chaotic existence that we all experience. And when we listen to music we hear that harmony, and I think that's what brings us the kind of serenity or peace or spirituality that is often missing in our lives.

I also agree with Dr. Wilson that we are all musical, but it depends very much on how it is taught. I was taught at a very young age, and I rebelled against it. I had an instructor who insisted I play classical music, and all I wanted to play was jazz. We didn't get along well at all. I finally ended up dropping the instruction because we used to fight every time. I wanted to play "Five Foot Two and Eyes of Blue" and he wanted me to play "The Blue Danube," or something of that nature.

So I agree with you that a lot depends on how it is taught. That also ties in to what the witnesses have been saying today—that it is important that we, in using this as therapy, understand how to use it, how to apply it, and what is the best type of music for a given individual. We didn't have time to really look into much of the work that you have done, Dr. Clair, in terms of seeing the dramatic responses, but I assume for all the therapists—and I assume that most of those who were cheering in the audience a moment ago are engaged in music therapy of one kind or another—would agree that's something that we need to focus on—the special aspect of that kind of training.

I assume also, Dr. Wilson, that there may be some difference. You have touched upon music therapy as far as directing it toward children or young people, versus those that are older. Is there a basic difference in that kind of therapy?

Dr. WILSON. I would like to respond to your question by enlarging the concept of music therapy.

In a recent letter to Mr. Adelstein, Professor Roehman said both music education and music therapy are paths which converge on human wellness and vitality in later life. They, like Watson and Crick's double helix, can be two fundamental strands of a comprehensive, preventive, therapeutic model which provides pleasurable physical and mental activity, as well as social contact, for many of our senior citizens. This is true for children, as well.

I also want to call your attention to a video which was submitted to you which introduces another possibility for the use of music therapy. A patient who had a spinal cord tumor—who was a patient of mine—by all rights should be not only wheelchair bound, but bedridden. She is not only not wheelchair bound and bedridden, but rides a bicycle and uses on roller skates. She actually began her own music therapy program at the suggestion of a neurophysiologist at the University of California in Los Angeles who told her she really should be doing small, rhythmic exercises for short periods of time. Having been a string bass player before, she said, "Well, that sounds like music to me." She made her own exercises up, and despite the fact that her brain is in essence disconnected from the lower spinal cord, she looks to all practical purposes to be completely normal.

Now, if that's the case—to respond to your question to Dr. Lee, Senator Reid—in terms of economics, if what we learn from this patient could be applied to the enormous population of younger people with spinal cord injuries, the savings through restoration of some kind of mobility would be simply incalculable.

At our recent conference at the University of Rochester we had an early report from a music therapist who has taken the plunge into studying neurophysiology and now works with patients with spinal cord injuries using musical stimulation. So, research has begun on this potentially very important use of music therapy which simply does not respect the question specifically of age.

Another point I would like to just add—because this is my own experience—concerns the relative newness and unfamiliarity of music therapy in general hospitals. I was responsible for the introduction of music therapy into the hospital where I work in California simply by inviting a music therapist to participate in the hospice program, whose patients who are being cared for for malignancies. Interestingly, there was no resistance to her joining the staff because she wasn't competing with anyone. The sad story is that when patients have fatal illnesses, the doctors are often out of town, so to speak. I'm sorry to say that about my profession, but the fact is that that happens.

Music therapists working with hospice patients make a very significant contribution to patient care. A patient with a malignant brain tumor, who was my own patient and who was being seen by the music therapist, had finally withdrawn from all communication not only with me, but with his family.

The music therapist was able to reach him, to draw him out. I remember the last interview that I had with him was one in which a question about whether he should have a second round of chemotherapy was raised. Instead of simply sitting there as though he was not a participant, he became very emotional. Even though he had lost the ability to communicate meaningfully with language, he was able to indicate exactly what it was that he wanted.

So he actually was brought back into the family/physician/patient interaction in a very important way.

We really haven't begun to scratch the surface. We have not begun to see really what the basic physiology of music is. I think that I'd like to have a conversation with Mickey Hart about where the rhythmic impulse comes from because, in fact, the leading edge of neurophysiologic research now has to do with the generation of rhythmic activity in the brain, and it influence on thought, consciousness, and movement.

I see a very happy future. I think that you gentlemen and ladies in the Congress and Senate could help a great deal by simply legitimizing this effort and the concept.

Senator COHEN. Thank you very much, Dr. Wilson.

We're nearing the end of the hearing, itself, but I wanted to say how helpful this has been.

I remember years ago when it came to dealing with the elderly the solution was simply to put people in nursing homes. At that time, I recall Senator Percy, who was serving in the Senate at that time, referred to warehousing the dying. There was very little being done at that time in trying to stimulate the elderly, but rather just to put them where it would be convenient for their relatives to visit them and to care for them physically, but not enough was being done for the spiritual side or the physical side.

There was too much dependency upon drugs to kill the pain in dealing with their particular problems, or to keep them quiet, or whatever. That led to a series of investigations by the Aging Committee, as such, or a Senate committee, as well as the House, and the forming of a House Select Committee on Aging, as well as one in the Senate.

I think we have come quite a long way since that time in just dealing not only with physical rehabilitation, but we have come to a different level, or we are coming to a different level now, and that's to see the importance of the mental side, the spiritual side, and the role that not only music, but the entire field of meditation—they are doing quite a vast array of experiments now in terms of finding out what role the mind plays in curing disease or helping to cure disease.

So we've got a whole new universe of experience that has to be explored yet, and I think this hearing has been particularly helpful.

As you asked, Dr. Wilson, and others have asked: what can we do? We can help give it credibility, but our own credibility rests upon the quality of the people that come before us, and so we thank all of you for coming and being part of the panel here to lend credibility to this inquiry into new and very productive ways of dealing with our elderly.

Senator REID. Thank you, Senator Cohen.

This concludes the hearing today. It has been a first in many ways. We are going to have another first. I'm going to ask Ken Medema, an experienced performer, as we know, and a music therapist, to conclude this hearing with a song summarizing what we have heard. I believe this is the first hearing in U.S. Senate history to conclude with a musical coda.

Go ahead and make history.

[Musical presentation by Mr. Medema.]

Mr. MEDEMA [singing]:

I'm growing old and help me stay young.
Let the music be played.
Let the songs now be sung.
Back in Indiana,
We never really did know,
There were folks like music therapists, round,
Such a thing to learn today.
I had a stroke.
Look at me now.
I learned to play the music somehow.
Whoever thought we'd see it,
In the halls of Congress today,
There is music playing and songs being sung,
It must be the start of something brand new,
So I'm growing old
Help me stay
Forever Young.

[Whereupon, at 1:25 p.m., the committee adjourned, to reconvene at the call of the Chair.]

APPENDIX

Item 1

Testimony of
Pinchas Zukerman
Before the
Special Committee on Aging
United States Senate
Hearing on
"Forever Young: Music and Aging"
August 1, 1991

"I have been intensely involved with music all of my life.
In my experience, most music becomes a bonding force to unite
and often to comfort people and lead them to some kind of
emotional healing. It helps provide a way to celebrate, to
grieve, to participate in the fundamental thoughts and feelings
that make us human. It provides a connection throughout
history. In Tchaikosvky's famous "1812 Overture" a dramatic
experience is related of living through a war where the Russians
were fending off Napoleon's advancing army. It is an amazing
thing that the war itself ended but the experience lives on
through the music.

All sound is an influence of some sort whether it is great
classical music or the noise on a city street. Human beings,
seem to be affected by sound more than anything else. I've read
studies of babies still in the womb reacting to sounds, and of
people near death who upon awakening can recount things they
heard while supposedly unconscious. When you know what the
beneficial results of certain sounds are, it is useful to become
attuned to those sounds. This is what the various music therapy
programs provide -- putting some attention on sounds that
influence us in a healing way. I have played in senior citizens
centers and this always seemed to give them an incredible "up."
I think somehow it activated an innate vitality that allowed
them a way to be truly engaged in life. If used properly, music
is certainly a powerful therapeutic tool. I personally know
several psychotherapists who use music in their work. One of
them told me she has used my performance of the Beethoven Violin
Concerto in her work with great success. She told me it created
a better environment for the patient and also allowed her to
become a better conduit for a therapeutic experience to occur.
So, I would say absolutely that music has an impact on a
person's physical, emotional, and mental functioning.

There are countless musicians that have continued their
careers into old age becoming some of the most revered artistic
names of our time -- Arthur Rubinstein, Vladimir Horowitz,
Leonard Bernstein, Rudolf Serkin, Claudio Arrau, Pablo Casals,
are just a very few of these names. The pianist Mieczyslaw
Horszowski (pronounced Meesloff Horshofskee) is now well into
his 90's and still touring around the world to the delight of
audiences of all ages. Remaining an active performer, which I
hope to do for a long time, just makes life better.

It is very important for serious consideration to be given
to including music therapy in quality care for older people. If
this isn't part of such programs, we will see a dwindling away
of older people and the effect will be to lose all their
knowledge from a life of experiences. It is imperative to pass
these things on. Older people are like seeds for the young.
They plant their knowledge and there is a continuation into the
next generation and the next, which is what builds a great
civilization.

I'm sorry I couldn't be in Washington to speak personally
about this subject which is so close to my heart. I hope this
testimony will be useful in helping to put attention on
something so important but which is often sadly neglected, or
worse, taken for granted."

Item 2

Department of Music,
Theatre, and Dance
Fort Collins, Colorado 80523
(303) 491-5529

Testimony
before the Senate Special Committee
on Aging

"Forever Young. Music and Aging".

by

Dr. Michael H. Thaut RMT
Associate Professor of Music Therapy
Director of Graduate Studies in Music Therapy
Director of Music Neurophysiology Research Laboratory
Colorado State University

Music in Motor Recovery with Neurological Disorders

Our research and clinical observations over the last 3 years clearly show that music can play an eminent role in the motor recovery of neurological disorders, e.g. stroke, parkinsons disease, closed head injuries, etc. Our data show that auditory stimulation can excite and shape activity in the motor system and thus can help to organize, sequence, pace and integrate complex movement. We have to emphasize that the primary clinical importance of music does not lie in its emotional or motivational value to accompany therapy but in its neurological effect to improve motor control.

In the following examples we try to outline different angles in which music is efficient as neurological technique to improve motor control. At Colorado State University we have done several studies to look at the effect of rhythm as pacing signal on muscle activity in arm extension/flexion and walking. We have found that when muscle activity is synchronized to auditory rhythm it becomes more regular and efficient. In other words, the timing of muscle activity (as measured by Electromyography) becomes more consistent and predictable. At the same time, duration of certain muscle groups (for example the calf muscle in walking) is shortened. However, during this more precise and shortened period of muscle activity the muscles work with a higher amplitude, i.e., more muscle fibers are activated.

These data strongly suggest that rhythmic pacing provides stronger and more focused muscular effort on a neurological level, which translates into improved motor control, e.g., better rhythmivity, during movement. We found these effects with normal individuals and persons with stroke, cerebellar dysfunction, and motor planning disorder. Our findings lead us to believe, that rhythm is an excellent entrainment stimulus to retrain muscular control in individuals with damaged motor systems. Walking re-training to metronome bursts and musical stimulation has been incorporated into therapy protocols with great success into the clinical work we are doing.

Several other clinical examples underscore how efficient music can be to establish and re-train motor control. A 64 year old lady with massive diffuse brain damage due to a closed head injury sustained in a car accident had shown almost no purposeful fine or gross motor movement. She has had some piano training in her younger years. After the therapist had done some repatterning of her fingers on the keyboard she started moving her fingers independently, playing scales with both hands. She adjusted automatically her slumped posture and nonfunctional arm and wrist position in her wheelchair. She also opened her eyes to track her fingers moving and began to imitate finger patterns modeled by the therapist. Her display of motor skill and sensory-motor integration on the keyboard was dramatically out of proportion with her general level of functioning. The motor traces laid by her previous musical training were still intact and opened a window to re-training purposeful movement.

A 67 year old man who suffered from brain damage due to prolonged loss of oxygen during a heart attack was completely disoriented to time, place, or person. He did not recognize or remember even the most familiar things. His short term memory was also virtually nonexistent. However, when the therapist played the first notes of songs he once knew on the keyboard, the patient was consistently able to play and sing the songs with no help. Initially, the patient could not name the songs he just had sung nor could he remember his performance even in short term memory. Eventually, this activity became an excellent avenue to train his memory recall. The same patient walked exceedingly slow and showed no ability to initiate stopping or going on his own. With rhythmic pacing the patient was able to double his walking speed within the same session. Music on or off was also quickly comprehended as a signal for motor initiation without verbal cueing.

The examples above illustrate a striking clinical observation that musical traces in motor and cognitive memory are often preserved in a very severely damaged brain. This observation leads us to suggest that the musical modality is a very efficient modality to learn to perform and control very intricate movements in a neurologically deeply ingrained manner. Observing the rapid finger movements of a pianist illustrates this point very well. Would the pianist be able to learn and flawlessly perform the same sequences of finger motions without hearing himself. The likely answer is no. Again, therefore, organized sound as peripheral feedback for movement seems to have a very beneficial effect on creating motor memory.

The efficiency of music as neurological movement organizer in motor rehabilitation is not limited to accessing healthy motor schemes in patients with previous musical background. Our research which was done with nonmusicians bears that out. We have treated many nonmusician patients where the musical/rhythmic organization of movement, be it through musical pacemaking or through actually playing simple instruments to create your own acoustic feedback, has shown to re-train movement more efficiently than any other modality. Rhythmic organization of movement has helped to override tremors in the upper extremities during simple activities as reaching and lifting a cup. We have used musical stimuli as sensory trigger cues for weightshifting, balance control and motor initiation with Parkinson's disease patients.

Our clinical and resarch evidence shows that music - as extremely efficient modality to train motor control in healthy individuals -can be applied to re-train damaged motor control systems in neurological patients when properly adjusted and executed, such as by trained music therapists.

Based on the promising results we are seeing we believe that strong research efforts in music therapy and in interdisciplinary cooperation with rehabilitation medicine and neurophysiology are in order and fruitful. Applied research should look into the refinement of musical/rhythmic techniques in rehabilitation efforts with different clinical populations. However, we also feel a great need for basic neurophysiological research to elucidate the interaction between peripheral acoustic sensory input and motor neural activity.

Item 3

STANFORD UNIVERSITY SCHOOL OF MEDICINE
DIVISION OF GERONTOLOGY
Older Adult and Family Research and Resource Center

Mailing address:

Gerontology Research Programs
Mail code: 182C / MP
Veterans Administration Medical Center
3801 Miranda Avenue
Palo Alto, CA 94304

(415) 858-3989
(415) 493-5000 ext. 2011

THE IMPACT OF MUSIC THERAPY ON OLDER AMERICANS

EXPERT TESTIMONY
by Suzanne B. Hanser, Ed.D., RMT-BC
for the U.S. Senate Special Committee on Aging

August 1, 1991

AUTONOMY   EFFICACY   EMPOWERMENT
This is what music therapy offers older Americans!

AUTONOMY
Music is something which engages people, whether they are healthy and talented or disabled and dependent. While performing in an ensemble or listening to familiar, calming music, individuals are successful and creative, expressing themselves in a positive and unique way. This leads to a sense of **independence** for the many Americans who have difficulty coping with the problems associated with aging.

My recent research, sponsored by the National Institute on Aging, demonstrated that an 8-week music listening program facilitated by a music therapist could help clinically depressed, homebound older adults cope with stress and **overcome symptoms of anxiety, depression and physical complaints.** Using a controlled experimental design, these older individuals maintained statistically significant improvements on all standardized psychological tests over a nine-month period. This low-cost and easily accessible program holds potential for delaying or minimizing the need for residential care for this more frail population (see *Journal of Applied Gerontology*).

In other experimental research, I found that familiar music helped hospitalized patients relax and distracted them from pain. **Coping with pain and anxiety with minimal medication** was an outcome of this music therapy program in which patients were shown how to focus on the music, induce deep, rhythmic breathing and peaceful imagery.(see *Journal of Music Therapy*). More effective coping may lead to shorter hospital stays, faster recovery, and prevention of placement in skilled nursing facilities.

My NIA-sponsored music therapy research indicated that family caregivers of people with Alzheimer's disease experienced **relief from the stress and burden of caregiving** while involved in shared musical activities with their impaired loved ones. **Because even victims in the latest stages of Alzheimer's disease can appreciate and participate actively in music activities**, all family members are able to focus on more positive aspects of their loved one's personality and share in an enjoyable creative time together (see *Music and the Healing Process*). This program enabled families to adapt to the difficulties of caregiving at home, potentially delaying institutionalization of the person with Alzheimer's disease.

EFFICACY
As shown in many studies and clinical cases, music increases self-esteem. When older Americans engage in music activities, they derive a sense of self-esteem which affects their attitudes and approach to life. An enhanced sense of self-efficacy may lead to better functioning which, in the long run, improves mental and physical health.

Everyone is capable of creative expression, even those who respond to nothing else. Research by Dr. Mary Boyle demonstrates responsiveness to music by comatose patients. Other scientific evidence by Dr. Alicia Clair, Dr. William Beatty, myself and others provides documentation of amazing changes in cognitively impaired older Americans, particularly those with Alzheimer's and Parkinson's disease, when they are involved in music.

EMPOWERMENT
What does this research mean?
Music therapy empowers people to:
   *gain control over their moods, their futures, their lives
   *prevent or delay placement in long-term care facilities
   *remain independent, content and self-sufficient
   *identify their abilities and talents rather than concentrating on their worries and difficulties
   *have access to a cost-effective means of treatment which may benefit both physical and mental health

104

Statement of

John E. Frohnmayer

Chairman, National Endowment for the Arts

Chairman, National Council on the Arts

Hearing before the

Special Committee on Aging

United States Senate

on "Forever Young: Music and Aging"

August 1, 1991

Music knows no age. Vladimir Horowitz played the piano with
subtle beauty and skill when he was well over 80. At age 74,
Dizzy Gillespie continues to wow audiences with his virtuoso
jazz trumpet; and his contemporary, Isaac Stern, recently
returned to the stage in Israel to play the violin as a signal
for courage during the missile attacks in Tel Aviv. Ella
Fitzgerald, 73 years young, continues to captivate audiences
with her interpretations of Cole Porter's memorable music.
Dozens of composers, conductors, and musicians continue to
strive to perfect their art long past the typical retirement age.

Audiences, likewise, are not bound by the strictures of age. In
concert halls, opera houses, jazz clubs, and other venues, you
are likely to find a significant portion of the audience
composed of men and women over age 55. Older audiences bring
experience, appreciation, and understanding of the rich
complexities of music -- what Longfellow calls, the "universal
language of mankind".

For those older Americans who do not have easy access to live
musical performances, the Endowment has a number of programs
which help bring music to the people. As part of our overall
mission, the Endowment encourages greater access to and
participation in the arts in the belief that exposure to
artistic experiences contributes to the quality of life for all
citizens. Through grants awarded to individuals and
organizations, as well as its own programming, the Arts
Endowment ensures the continued involvement of older adults as
creative artists, students, volunteers, audience members, and
patrons.

To that end, the Arts Endowment's Music Program guidelines require all performing and presenting organizations to submit statements detailing their outreach efforts to the elderly and other special constituencies, such as the disabled and the underserved. Organizations that document significant activity or progress in this area score higher in the panel review process than those that do not. In addition, a significant number of Fellowship grants are awarded to older composers and performers each year on the basis of artistic excellence. For example, the Jazz Masters Fellowships which recognize significant, life-long achievement in jazz, were awarded this year to Clark Terry, age 71, Buck Clayton, age 80, Danny Barker, age 82, and Andy Kirk, age 93.

Our Music and Opera-Musical Theater Programs provide support to dozens of orchestras and opera companies which provide free or discounted tickets for older and disabled persons around the country. Some companies, such as the Fort Wayne Philharmonic, promote tour ensembles to senior centers, hospitals and parks. Also, OPERA America helps member opera companies make opera more accessible to all through an Endowment grant. In addition, our Folk Arts and Inter-Arts Programs fund a number of musical projects that benefit older Americans. Radio and television programs funded by our Media Arts Program enable millions of older Americans to enjoy the best in all forms of music.

Here are some additional examples of the types of projects we support:

> For the past 14 years, the Visiting Artists program in Davenport has allowed artists in Iowa and Illinois to share their talents with the elderly, with school children, factory workers, and persons with disabilities. These residencies are carried out in nearly 30 school districts and six area colleges as well as dozens of workplace, community center, and health care facilities. Each artist makes two or three appearances daily, and the residencies are a combination of performance and discussion. At the end of the residency, a full public concert is presented free of charge in one of several local theaters. In 1990-91, Visiting Artists will present 276 performances by 24 nationally recognized artists throughout the greater Quad City region, reaching an estimated 80,000 people.

The Ohio Chamber Orchestra received a $10,000 grant from the Music Program to support expansion of their summer series in Cleveland's Cain Park. This series makes classical music readily accessible to families and people on fixed incomes. Through arrangements with area retirement communities, transportation to and from concerts is provided for senior citizens.

The Dallas Symphony received a grant from the Music Program to support their classical subscription series, Super Pops Series, and community services. Under the **Heartstrings** program, senior citizens and people with physical and economic handicaps are given free season subscriptions.

A Folk Arts grant of $15,000 went to the Vermont Folklife Center to support "The Family Farm," a radio series of 50 five-minute programs about rural artists and art forms, including poetry, storytelling, songs, musical instruments, and wood and metal working that will reach out to 100,000 people. During the preparation for this series, the fieldworker interviewed over 125 farm households. After the program was broadcast over Vermont Public Radio, it was made available to National Public Radio as well as commercial radio stations.

In Omaha, Nebraska, the Metropolitan Arts Council (a 1990 Challenge grantee) is reaching out to everyone; their mission statement reads: ". . .we believe the arts are for all of us; for children and adults, for people of all races and ethnic backgrounds, for people with disabilities, and for people in hospitals and nursing homes."

We share their commitment to all audiences. Attached is a list of other selected projects which reflect the breadth and diversity of these programs for older Americans across the country.

The arts help us express some of our deepest feelings -- of love, trust, alienation, and hope. Art teaches us to verify our most personal experiences; to listen to intuition along with reason; and to perceive what is beyond the obvious. To develop in each person a sense of worth, of self-esteem through the ability to command self-expression in the arts, is a task which we Americans -- young and old, black and white, rich and poor -- face together as we near the beginning of a new century and a new age.

Selected Projects Involving Music and the Aging

Horizon Concerts, Inc. (New York, NY) presents a series of concerts for audiences who, due to age or infirmity, are unable to travel to concert halls. Concerts in homes for the elderly has been the focus of Horizon's programs since its inception in 1975.

Downtown Music Productions (New York, NY) performs a concert for the JASA Community Senior Center as part of a series of educational events on women composers and chamber music. In addition, the Downtown Duo (flute and piano) has been performing special programs for the elderly in hospitals and nursing homes throughout New York's five boroughs.

Arioso Wind Quintet (San Diego, CA) performs a concert at the Mt. Miguel Covenant Village, a retirement community.

Sea Cliff Chamber Players (Sea Cliff, NJ) presents one of its four concert series at reduced prices for senior citizens and other special constituencies.

Dale Warland Singers (Minneapolis, MN) provides free and discounted tickets to seniors and offers discounts in cooperation with a variety of senior-care medical and insurance plans.

Milwaukee Symphony (Milwaukee, WI) provides complimentary tickets to Artreach Milwaukee which distributes them to agencies serving the elderly and other special constituencies. Milwaukee Symphony also performs two free senior citizen concerts each year.

Music of the Baroque Concert Series (Chicago, IL) offers discounts of up to 50% to senior citizens for either subscription or single concert tickets.

Musica Sacra, Inc. (New York, NY) donates unsold or returned tickets to the elderly through senior citizen homes and facilities.

San Francisco Chanticleer, Inc. (San Francisco, CA) makes available approximately 50 free tickets to senior citizen groups and a variety of social service organizations for 12 self-produced Bay Area concerts each year through Performing Arts Services' Special Audiences program.

Canton Symphony (Canton, OH) sends its smaller ensembles to perform in nursing homes and at senior centers.

Flint Symphony Orchestra (Flint, MI) targets its Sunday Matinee Series to attract senior citizens to its concerts.

Fort Wayne Philharmonic (Ft. Wayne, IN) sends a core group of 18 musicians to perform chamber orchestra and ensemble concerts in senior citizen centers.

Lexington Philharmonic (Lexington, KY) has its chamber orchestra perform in retirement homes in the area.

Lincoln Symphony (Lincoln, NE) makes its concerts more accessible to low-income senior citizens by providing free transportation to the concert hall on the evenings of the performances.

Stamford Symphony (Stamford, CT) issues discounted and free tickets to senior citizens for its Great Artists Performance Series.

Musical Arts Association (The Cleveland Orchestra) (Cleveland, OH) schedules eight daytime concerts, the Friday Matinee Series, at reduced rates for those who find it difficult to attend evening concerts due to financial or travel limitations. The orchestra also provides group sales of tickets by special arrangement.

San Francisco Symphony (San Francisco, CA) provides subscription tickets at a pre-concert rate of $4. Its program, Seniors to the Symphony, provides transportation for over 2,000 limited income and handicapped citizens through community organizations. The Symphony also arranges bus service to the matinee concerts from 37 Bay Area locations to assist seniors and others.

South Carolina Symphony (Columbia, SC) makes it possible for the elderly and handicapped in nursing homes, who are unable to attend concerts, to meet visiting guest artists and hear them perform.

Santa Barbara Symphony (Santa Barbara, CA) developed its "Informances" project in 1983 which was originally funded by the Endowment under the Model Demonstration Projects category. Informances are 30 minute concert previews by sight-impaired docent from the Braille Institute and two orchestra musicians who provide, a week before the Sunday Matinee concert, a lecture/demonstration visit in senior resident centers.

Phoenix Symphony (Phoenix, AZ) performs in retirement communities in the greater metropolitan area. Senior citizen discounts are available and complimentary tickets are distributed to senior citizen groups.

Chicago String Ensemble (Chicago, IL) offers senior citizens free admittance to its dress rehearsals where the conductor speaks with the audience and answers questions during the breaks.

Grand Rapids Symphony (Grand Rapids, MI) presents ensemble performances in senior citizen facilities and provides amplifiers for the hearing impaired for subscription concerts in DeVos Hall.

Long Beach Symphony (Long Beach, CA) sponsors 12 "Informances" or musical recitals by its musicians in senior citizen homes, hospitals, and disabled veterans facilities.

Minnesota Orchestra (Minneapolis, MN) offers rehearsals and a special Saturday concert free of charge to approximately 3,000 senior citizens. They hear lectures and enjoy free refreshments prior to each event.

Jacksonville Symphony (Jacksonville, FL) offers ensemble performances in nursing homes and senior citizen centers, provides bus transportation to performances and subsidized tickets for low-income seniors, and presents pre-concert discussions prior to all Masterworks Concerts designed to serve visually-impaired people.

Louisville Orchestra (Louisville, KY) makes accessible to senior citizens preferring daytime events a nine-concert series called the Cumberland Coffee Concerts, and provides shuttle buses throughout the city.

Item 5

Testimony Presented before

U. S. Senate Special Committee on Aging

Gail B. Broder, RMT-BC
The Westchester House, St. Louis, Missouri

My career as a clinical music therapist working with older adults really began with the lessons I learned from my own family. I grew up surrounded by the warmth of a large, close-knit extended family which included all four grandparents and eight great aunts and uncles. All of them were vibrant, energetic, vital people who lived their lives to the fullest. They taught me a lesson about the value of the elderly, for I always saw their contributions to each other, to our family, and to the community. Throughout their lives they loved music - whether listening to the radio, listening to records, playing their instruments, attending concerts, or sitting around the kitchen table with cups of coffee singing the Yiddish melodies of their youth. Music added something to their lives that enriched them, and, through their example, it enriched me. From these early experiences with my family, I chose to focus my work as a music therapist in the area of older adults. This testimony will briefly outline my clinical practice of music therapy with this population.

Let me begin by citing several case studies from my clinical work at The Westchester House Retirement Center. The first case involved an eighty four year old woman who I will refer to as Margaret. Margaret had suffered a severe stroke localized in her right hemisphere resulting in complete paralysis on her left side and aphasia. Her speech loss was complete and, when I began working with her, three months of speech therapy had yielded little result. Her voice was barely more than a whisper and she was able to only mumble one or two syllables to express basic needs. This communication was very frustrating for her, and she often cried through these brief exchanges. Her daughters told me of her love for music and how they had sung together at family gatherings. I initially saw Margaret to establish her interest in music listening experiences. On my first visit, I explained my reason for coming and informed her that I had brought a variety of tapes with me which I planned to play in the hopes that she could nod to the selections she liked. This seemed acceptable to Margaret and she smiled. I inserted the first tape, a Mitch Miller sing along collection, and the first song, "Shine on Harvest Moon", began. Spontaneously, Margaret began to sing the song in full voice. Though her diction was poor, words could be distinguished. After follow-up consultation with her speech therapist and neurologist, it was determined that though the brain had been affected in the speech area, there was apparently no damage to the primary section that mediates singing, a portion of the brain separate from the speech areas. In continuing music therapy sessions, I worked with Margaret to re-open her lines of communication by helping her to sing her requests and responses. This work was successful resulting in a decrease in frustration during attempts to communicate.

The second case study of a client I will refer to as Anna is an excellent example of how music can enrich the lives of the "well" older adults. At age 92, Anna initiated her own placement to the nursing home following her husband's death as she did not wish to be a burden to her only child. Anna was mentally alert and oriented with her primary complaint being arthritis pain which impaired her mobility. Though she experienced cataract removal and a lens implant, overall Anna presented as an essentially healthy, alert individual. She quickly became involved in all aspects of the music program in the nursing home. Anna became the song leader of hymns at the protestant religious services and attended every sing along, music groups, and program featuring a guest musician. When she was in her room, Anna would often hum to herself or listen to the radio. Being very modest, she was quick to brush off compliments with a smile, usually indicating that what she lacked in quality she made up for in volume. She reports that her involvement in music

2

is the key factor that keeps her alert, healthy and happy because she feels useful and involved. Anna's health continues to be excellent and her level of musical involvement remains high.

These case studies help to illustrate some of the underlying theoretical principles of music therapy intervention with older adults. First, music motivates overall participation, reaching even the most regressed, unresponsive patient. Because the auditory nerve bundle first enters the brain at the level of the brain stem, music stimulates brain activity even when the individual can not give an overt response. Secondly, music serves to reinforce general reality orientation by extending the time that patients can functionally participate in the here and now. Because music is a temporal art (based on regular pulse occurring over time), response to the real stimulus of music occurring in the environment allows individuals to function in the present moment. Thirdly, music is a natural social activity that allows for communication, group functioning, and interpersonal interactions. A fourth theoretical principle of music therapy involves the emotional nature of music. We have learned to associate emotion with music, making it a natural vehicle for expression of feelings so necessary for older individuals dealing with the losses associated with aging. A fourth factor is the ability of music to stimulate movement and exercise, distract from pain, and encourage more physical activity which has a positive impact on physical health of older adults.[1] Finally, even patients with severe disabilities such as dementia can have a high capacity for functioning in music creating opportunities for more natural interactions with family members and improving their overall quality of life.[2]

In drawing these remarks to a close, I would like to make some comments about the future use of music therapy services for older individuals. The elderly population continues to grow rapidly while there is a continuing shortage of health care workers trained to work with this population. The people currently admitted to nursing homes have more serious physical and mental impairments than in the past. Though the need is great and music therapy is an efficacious therapeutic modality with older adults, professional music therapists are not entering this work force for simple financial reasons. Given the low reimbursement rates of Medicaid to nursing home facilities and the lack of Medicare reimbursement for music therapy services, many long term care facilities cannot afford to hire a music therapist. Home care agencies will not usually provide a non-reimbursable service, and families burdened by escalating medical costs can not afford services that are not covered. Without reimbursement, older adults will be denied music therapy services that could have significant impact on the mental and physical functioning of older adults. It is my hope that Congress will address the issue of Medicare reimbursement for music therapy services so that older adults can avail themselves of this therapy.

---

1. Douglass, Donna. (1981). **Accent on Rhythm**. Salem, OR: LaRoux Enterprises, Inc.
2. Bright, Ruth. (1988). **Music Therapy in the Dementias: Improving the Quality of Life**. St. Louis, MO: MMB Music, Inc.

Item 6

National Association for Music Therapy, Inc.

8455 COLESVILLE ROAD   SILVER SPRING, MD 20910   (301) 589-3300   FAX (301) 589-5175

Testimony

U. S. Senate Special Committee on Aging
Hearing - "Forever Young: Music and Aging"

Submitted by

Barbara J. Crowe, RMT-BC
Associate Professor of Music Therapy, Arizona State University
President, National Association for Music Therapy

On Thursday, August 1, 1991, The U. S. Senate Special Committee on Aging is holding an historic hearing entitled, "Forever Young: Music and Aging". For the first time in Senate history, the committee will hear testimony about the benefits of music as a specific therapeutic modality used to regain and maintain physical and mental health, and positively influence the quality of life for our older citizens. Music therapy is defined as the use of music interventions specifically selected by a board certified music therapist to accomplish the restoration, maintenance and/or improvement of social or emotional functioning, mental processing, and/or physical health.

Though there is a great deal of historical precedent for the use of music as a therapeutic, healing tool, the profession of music therapy was established in the United States in the late 1930's and early 1940's when musicians and music teachers were utilized in psychiatric hospitals to provide a unique form of therapy. During and after the Second World War, the Veteran's Administration Hospitals employed music specialists to provide services to the large number of veterans who required physical and psychological rehabilitation. By the early 1950's, a new therapeutic discipline had emerged and the early practitioners recognized the need for formal education and research into the use of music as a therapeutic modality. With the establishment of the National Association for Music Therapy in 1950, this process began.

Today, music therapy is a well-established, research based profession. Over 4000 music therapists across the country use carefully selected music activity interventions in the treatment and rehabilitation of children and adults (including older individuals) with a wide spectrum of physical, psychological, and social needs and including individuals from the entire spectrum of ethnic, demographic, and social backgrounds.

The scope of music therapy practice and services is broad because music is a motivating, flexible activity on which to base a therapeutic interaction. The professional music therapist is well trained in assessing client functioning and needs, determining appropriate behavioral, social, educational or rehabilitative goals, and in devising appropriate music activity interventions to achieve the stated goals. The professional music therapist has completed a curriculum in one of sixty five post-secondary institutions of learning with a degree program in music therapy approved by a national association of music therapy and holds an exam-based board certification conferred by the Certification Board for Music Therapy, Inc.

Music therapists are currently employed in nursing homes and day programs for older individuals, in hospitals and community programs for the emotionally disturbed of all ages, in substance abuse rehabilitation, in pre-school early intervention programs for children at risk, in special education programs in public school systems, in centers and hospitals for the rehabilitation of head-trauma patients, in prison systems, in educational programs for the developmentally delayed, and in general hospitals. Music therapy is an efficacious, cost-effective means of meeting the health and rehabilitative needs of a large segment of our population.

Music is a powerful tool. When utilized by a certified professional music therapist, it can make the difference between withdrawal and awareness in an Alzheimer's patient, immobility and rhythmic gait in a stroke victim, depression and healthy grieving in a new widow, or loneliness and social participation in a new nursing home resident.

Because hearing is the first sense to develop and the last to fade as we die, we respond to sound, especially the organized sound that is music, in inherent, intense and profound ways. Anyone who has observed a baby as young as six months old moving in beat to a rhythmic dance tune or who has seen a grandparent flooded by memories when they hear a long forgotten song recognizes that music can have powerful effects on people.

In a recent study on stress reported in Newsweek, 75% of the adults polled stated they used music as their primary means of stress reduction. Instinctively, we humans recognize the therapeutic value of music. The professional music therapist is specifically trained in both music and the behavioral sciences so that they can systematically use music activities and interventions as the basis of the required therapy or rehabilitation. Music therapy interventions for older adults illustrates this process. When dealing with preventative health issues for the well older individual, music interventions can be used to stimulate social interaction and effective communication. Involvement in music can help maintain physical and mental functioning while supporting healthy expression of emotions. In work with the infirmed older patient, music therapy services provide reality orientation for dementia patients because music provides a real, obvious stimulus that is clearly measured in time. The highly rhythmic aspects of music can also help stroke patients regain smooth walking gait. Alzheimer's patients have been found to respond well to music decreasing their agitation and allowing the emergence of pre-disease personality traits and memory. Carefully selected songs stimulate memory and allow the individual to do required life-review. Participation in music stimulates interpersonal interaction, provides a time structured event that successfully focuses attention on the environment, makes physical movement more motivating and less painful and stimulates mental processes especially memory.

The U. S. Senate hearing, "Forever Young: Music and Aging" has focused particular attention on music therapy services for older adults. Three specific areas that can potentially be impacted by this hearing are increased awareness of music therapy as a valid, efficacious health care service to older Americans, appropriations for research and demonstration projects and changes in Federal regulations that effect delivery of services to older adults. Specific areas of concern are outlined as follows:

1. **Increased awareness of music therapy services for older adults**
   A. To raise general public awareness of music therapy services through media coverage.
   B. To increase awareness among legislative, governmental and regulatory bodies of the applications of music therapy.
   C. To raise the awareness of music therapy applications among professional health care colleagues.
   D. To make music therapy services and applications known to consumers who may wish to have music therapy as part of their total health care.

Although the modern profession of music therapy began in the late 1930's in the United States, these is still a pervasive lack of awareness of the existence of this professional discipline and its standards, practices and research. Public relation efforts need to be undertaken to increase the general awareness and acceptance of music therapy services in rural and urban setting and to make information concerning specific applications with various client groups including minority and low-income individuals more readily available. This will foster inclusion of music therapy in services for the people of all ages with special needs, thus providing an effective, unique treatment modality for many people and increasing employment opportunities for professionally trained music therapists.

2. **To have funds appropriated for music therapy research, special project grants, demonstration grants and contracts from the department of Health and Human Services, National Institute of Disability and Rehabilitation Research, and other related opportunities.**

   A. To have Congress, the Secretary of Education or others in a position of authority designate music therapy research and projects as eligible for funding with special projects money.

Though some research has been done to document the effectiveness of music therapy services, especially in meeting the specific needs of older adults, many areas of investigation need to be further explored. The efficacy of music therapy has been demonstrated through extensive clinical practice. Model demonstration projects, basic scientific research, and clinical outcome research can extend and further validate music therapy applications. **Demonstration projects** expand music therapy services to facilities offering services to older adults, their families and their communities. **Basic scientific research** may document specific neurological and physiological processes involving the influence of music on behavior. **Clinical outcome research** provides much needed evaluation of treatment effects.

A modest allocation of Federal funds would allow professional music therapists to make substantial progress in these needed areas of study.

3. **To influence legislation and regulation that impacts the availability of music therapy services to older Americans and other populations**

   A. To include language in the Older Americans Act or other appropriate legislation authorizing:
      1. demonstration projects focusing on music therapy in long-term care, senior centers, preventative health services, in-home services for frail individuals, intergenerational programs, programs to meet the special needs of minority and low-income older individuals and other programs for older Americans and their caretakers.
      2. education and training projects, including establishment of a non-degree equivalency program at a post-secondary institution of learning for retraining musicians for careers in music therapy with older adults.

   B. To have music therapy services included in the HCFA regulations:
      1. insert definition of music therapist as a qualified professional in the area of supportive services who is certified to effectively direct an ongoing program related to Quality of Life needs of the residents
      2. include music therapy in the specialized rehabilitative services section of the regulations (pending for 10 years)

   C. To have music therapy written into the new Federal regulations for adult day care facilities and services as a rehabilitative therapist.
   D. To have music therapy listed in the Medicare reimbursement guide.
   E. To have authorization in NIH, NIA and NIMH guidelines for music therapy research studies.
   F. To include music therapy services in other pertinent legislation and regulations.

Federal regulations and reimbursement guidelines set the standard for health care, educational and rehabilitative services in this country. It is in the best interest of the older adults and other individuals to eliminate any exclusionary language from these guidelines and include specific mention of music therapy in the outline of rehabilitative services so that client groups can be afforded the optimal choices for effective care.

I want to take this opportunity to thank the U.S. Senate Special Committee on Aging for holding this hearing on music and aging and focusing attention on music therapy services for this group. Thank you for the opportunity to comment on this topic.

Item 7

P	Philadelphia Developmental Disabilities Corporation
D	2350 West Westmoreland Street
D	Philadelphia, Pennsylvania 19140-4793
C	215-229-4550

E.-A. Gentile
Executive Vice President
Chief Operating Officer

Gerald Levinson, President
Albert Teti, Chairman

July 31, 1991

Members of the Senate Special Committee on Aging,

Enclosed is a copy of our Testimony to your Special Committee on Aging, submitted for August 1, 1991.

Thank you for recognizing the needs of seniors, and we ask that you remember, as well, all populations. Music transcends all ages, languages, cultures.

All seniors have special needs, and this holds true for people who have had special needs all their lives. The spectrum of services for developmentally disabled people must be complete -- early education, schooling, working and retirement.

PDDC/ARC began the first adult work training center, the first infant stimulation program and began the fight for Right to Education in Philadelphia. We have now had a Pilot Seniors Program for almost two years. You and any member of your staffs are cordially invited to visit this program at any time.

If you have any questions, I would be most happy to speak with you.

Sincerely,

E-A. Gentile, Executive Vice-President
Chief Operating Officer

TESTIMONY FOR SENATE AGING COMMITTEE HEARING
AUGUST 1, 1991 10:00AM - 1:00PM
DIRKSEN SENATE OFFICE BUILDING, WASHINGTON, D.C.
"FOREVER YOUNG: MUSIC AND AGING"

My name is Erman-Anthony Gentile. I am the Executive Director of the Philadelphia Chapter of the Association for Retarded Citizens and Executive Vice-President of the Philadelphia Developmental Disabilities Corporation which is incorporated as a service delivery system for developmentally disabled citizens in the Delaware Valley.

In 1948, we started the first workshop for retarded citizens in the City of Philadelphia and are now part of a nationwide service delivery system that provides work opportunities in both vocational developmental centers and the community for developmentally disabled citizens of working age.

Our agency is the oldest of 1500 ARC's in the United States, having been founded over forty years ago. I have been director for twenty years. This agency was responsible for the initial court litagation that resulted in the passage of Public Law 94-142: The Right to Education for All Handicapped Children. This agency started the first early intervention program for developmentally disabled infants that is now part of the service delivery system throughout the nation. Two years ago we established the Horowitz Cultural Center which provides courses for handicapped students of all ages in the Delaware Valley in the creative arts, i.e. art, printmaking, ceramics, music, handbells, dance, etc. using a college semester design. We have established the first Seniors Program for older developmentally disabled senior citizens in the City of Philadelphia.

Congress has seen in its wisdom the need for programs for developmentally disabled infants and handicapped school children. It recognizes the need for real work opportunities for developmentally disabled adults. Please, remember the senior citizen who is developmentally disabled, and who in many cases has not had the benefit of any early education or work experiences. They are truly the 'doubly devalued forgotten' population.

Over 11% of the general population is over 65 years of age. Of that 11% one to one-half million are estimated to be developmentally disabled. As the general population has been aging so has the handicapped population, at about the same rate. No planning for or provision of services have been designed for this emerging senior handicapped population either by the developmental disabilities service delivery system or the service delivery system for the aged. The literature is only just beginning to discuss this problem and few programs have been designed to address this need.

We at Philadelphia Developmental Disabilities Corporation have started and are expanding a model program to provide services for the community based senior citizen who is developmentally disabled. Other Philadelphia agencies are meeting with us to procure information on how they can also implement programs.

Music and Music Therapy have been found to be one of the most effective components of our program for this special senior citizen population. Our older adults are not only experiencing the physical and cognitive changes of aging but are doubly devalued by society because of being developmentally disabled. Our seniors have few family members who can advocate for them, limited social contacts and few social-recreational programs available to them. They are not accepted into Senior Citizen Centers because of deeply ingrained attitudes and beliefs. Senior Citizens in our society are already a devalued population and they do not want to be equated with "those people".

We have found that music activities and music therapy help our special seniors develop a social interaction and sharing with others that is much like that seen in a non-handicapped senior center. Music assists our special seniors to remember the past and stay in touch with the present. Music motivates physical activity and exercise and, perhaps most important, provides an outlet for creative self expression.

Let me share some vignettes with you about our special senior population, ages 55 and up:

Shirley is a member of our Seniors Program who lives at home with her elderly mother and handicapped sister. She has worked in our sheltered workshop for 33 years, sitting quietly at her work station doing bench work. She was described as shy and very withdrawn - a person who was easily frightened by new people and new experiences - afraid to look people directly in the eye. Music activities in the Seniors Program, such as song discussion, Name That Tune and instrumental music playing, have helped Shirley "blossom like a flower in spring". She smiles frequently, welcomes new members and visitors, and "talks your ear off."

Sydney was admitted to a state residential institution for the mentally retarded when he was ten years old. He spent 34 years of his life in that same institution before being placed in a community sheltered living situation. Sydney was the first member of the Seniors Program and found a place where he could express his fascination with music. He sings all the old songs, improvises on Orff instruments and is "the life of the party".

George had a very unstable childhood, never had a chance to learn to read, experienced trouble with the law and struggled with a drinking problem. His records consistently describe him as very dependent with an extremely poor self image. In the Fall of 1990, as a member of our sheltered workshop, he was enrolled in our Seniors Program where we discovered he had a previously unknown natural singing talent. Subsequently he auditioned and became a member of the Bright Hopes, an elite musical performing group sponsored by our agency whose members exhibit exceptional musical talent. His involvement with the Bright Hopes has given him a sense of pride in his achievements, a feeling of group membership and a sense of belonging. In previous years George was a consistent winner of gold medals for track in the local Special Olympics until a heart condition and deteriorating knees prevented his participation. His participation in music has filled a void in George's life and brought him even more acclaim. Weekly musical rehearsals with the Bright Hopes and participation in the Seniors Program are highlights in George's life.

These are but a sample of the vignettes that can be written for the over one million developmentally disabled senior citizens in the United States if programs like ours can be researched and replicated. The United Nations Declaration on the Rights of Disabled Persons states that such persons have the "same fundamental rights as their fellow-citizens of the same age, which implies first and foremost, the right to enjoy a decent life, as normal and full as possible" (United Nations, 1975, Art. 3).

Please, remember the senior citizen who is developmentally disabled. We can begin to meet their needs with music in programs for seniors with developmental disabilities. Music Therapy is an old idea that is teaching us much about the needs and nature of mankind as we explore, experience and research the effectiveness and the necessity of music in our lives -- and in the lives of all people of all ages and all walks of life.

Contact: Mr. E-A. Gentile
          Executive Vice-President & Chief Operating Officer
          Philadelphia Developmental Disabilities Corporation
             and ARC/Philadelphia
          2350 W. Westmoreland Street
          Philadelphia, PA. 19140
          215-229-4550

8/seniors

Item 8
Before the
Special Committee on Aging
United States Senate

Statement of Rev. Dan C. McCurry
Trauma Chaplain
Cook County Hospital
Chicago, Illinois

August 1, 1991

Mr. Chairman, Members of the Committee:

Senator Reid, I appreciate your invitation to submit testimony for this committee's hearing to examine the use of music as a healing tool. Since hearing is one of our first senses to develop in the womb and is our last sense to leave before death, your focus on healing music truly encompasses our entire life span. These tones, rhythms, melodies, words, songs and other components of our musical healing tool kit provide all health care givers, and especially music therapists, a vast array of treatment modalities for patients and their families. As trauma chaplain in Cook County Hospital, the nation's fifth largest public hospital, I have also seen music provide great healing for doctors, nurses, social workers and other health care givers as well.

Cook County Hospital, with its network of community clinics, has always served the poorest, and thus the sickest population of Chicago. Our in-patient and out-patient census, on any one day, will encompass a greater variety of physical and social ills than many medical practitioners will see in a lifetime. They come to us overwhelmed by illness. Experience quickly teaches the limits of our surgical and pharmacological tools without an array of other therapies to enlist the patient's own will-to-live. Rooted in the very rhythms of heartbeat and respiration, music, at Cook County Hospital, well serves these therapeutic needs.

Other scientists, physicians, professional musicians, music therapists, patients and their families will be providing to the committee the medical and case history basis for the strength of music as a healing tool. As a chaplain, I have witnessed the use of music as a treatment modality. I am not a music therapist. There is, unfortunately, no certified music therapist on our staff and to my knowledge the hospital has never employed a trained music therapist. In all cases, however, both the role of music and that of the chaplain, are considered but one part of the professional treatment *team*, subject to all of the hospital's protocols and procedures for patient care. The skills and training of professional music therapists are essential to draw upon the full range of benefits which music can provide to the health care team.

Gerontology Unit

Memorable music runs throughout the life experiences of our older generations and can be used to assist in their healthcare treatment today. Most prominent is its role in the treatment of the terminally and fatally ill patients in which an older population predominates. With both patient and family, each of the steps of grief and leave-taking can be addressed musically with demonstrably effective results. Music catalyzes many life events at this time. Its melodies evoke the strengths of past life fully lived with family and friends, its lyrics give voice to words of grief or joy that may be difficult to express at this time, its presence within the health care setting provides a continuity to a life which is being thought of primarily as something now at an end.

Equally important, music provides a tool kit of energetic memories to fuel the rehabilitation procedures of physical therapy and occupational therapy for seniors feeling burdened by bodies which don't respond as they once did. Wheelchair waltzes, the "Cook County Cake Walk", exercised to the "golden oldies" are available to patients at all levels of physical and mental acuity. Especially with seniors, music making, on a variety of instruments, is as crucial as musical response and listening.

Summary

Throughout Cook County Hospital, music is used in a wide variety of therapeutic ways with people of all ages. Music heals as it reaches through scar tissues of illness to touch the strengths of the imagination.

Thank you.

Dan McCurry can be reached at Ste. 2W, 5516 S. Cornell, Chicago, IL 60637
Tel: (312) 955-0197

Item 9

MUSIC THERAPY FOR OLDER AMERICANS ACT

Summary of Provisions Approved by the U.S. Senate

Senator Harry Reid introduced a bill, S. 1723, entitled the "Music Therapy for Older Americans Act" on September 18, 1991, based on the findings of the hearing of the Special Committee on Aging. The bill would amend the Older Americans Act to define music therapy, and to include music therapy both as a supportive service and a preventive health service. The bill would also authorize funding for music therapy research and demonstration projects, as well as education, training and information dissemination.

Most of the provisions of the bill were passed by the U.S. Senate on November 12, 1991, as part of an Older Americans Act reauthorization bill. On April 9, 1992, the House of Representatives passed all of the provisions approved by the Senate. At the time of this printing, a final version of the legislation had not yet been signed into law by the President.

The bill approved by the Senate and House includes music therapy in the following ways:

1) Defines music therapy as, "the use of musical or rhythmic interventions specifically selected by a music therapist to accomplish the restoration, maintenance or improvement of social or emotional functioning, mental processing, or physical health of an older individual."

2) Adds music therapy to a list of supportive services, such as home health and reader services, that are designed "to assist older individuals in avoiding institutionalization and to assist individuals in long-term care institutions who are able to return to their communities" These services are provided by state and area agencies on aging under state plans.

3) Adds music therapy to a list of services designed to enable older individuals "to attain and maintain physical and mental well-being."

4) Adds music therapy to a list of services designed to satisfy special needs and quality of life of older individuals, particularly those with greatest economic and social need.

5) Defines music therapy as a preventive health service, such as routine health screening and nutritional counseling.

6) Creates new demonstration and research projects that "advance the understanding of the efficacy and benefits of providing music therapy to older individuals."

7) Institutes education, training and information dissemination projects for music therapists about gerontology and for the aging network about music therapy.

ISBN 0-16-038346-3

9 780160 383465

90000